No More Theories Please!

A Guide for Elementary Teachers

L. K. MASAO

ROWMAN & LITTLEFIELD EDUCATION
Lanham • New York • Toronto • Plymouth, UK
2009

Published in the United States of America
by Rowman & Littlefield Education
A division of Rowman & Littlefield Publishers, Inc.
A wholly owned subsidiary of The Rowman & Littlefield Publishing Group, Inc.
4501 Forbes Boulevard, Suite 200, Lanham, Maryland 20706
www.rowmaneducation.com

Estover Road, Plymouth PL6 7PY, United Kingdom

Copyright © 2009 by L. K. Masao

This book was placed by the Educational Design Services LLC literary agency.

All rights reserved. No part of this publication may be reproduced, stored in a retrieval system, or transmitted in any form or by any means, electronic, mechanical, photocopying, recording, or otherwise, without the prior permission of the publisher.

British Library Cataloguing in Publication Information Available

Library of Congress Cataloging-in-Publication Data

Masao, L. K., 1975–
 No more theories please! : a guide for elementary teachers / L. K. Masao.
    p. cm.
 Includes bibliographical references and index.
 ISBN-13: 978-1-57886-989-3 (cloth : alk. paper)
 ISBN-10: 1-57886-989-7 (cloth : alk. paper)
 ISBN-13: 978-1-57886-990-9 (pbk. : alk. paper)
 ISBN-10: 1-57886-990-0 (pbk. : alk. paper)
 [etc.]
 1. Elementary school teaching—Handbooks, manuals, etc. I. Title.
 LB1555.M397 2009
 372.1102—dc22
                                                                    2008043715

∞™ The paper used in this publication meets the minimum requirements of American National Standard for Information Sciences—Permanence of Paper for Printed Library Materials, ANSI/NISO Z39.48-1992.
Manufactured in the United States of America

Contents

Foreword   vii
Lucretia Jackson

Introduction   ix

PART I: Organization

1   The Physical Organization of the Classroom   3

▪ centers ▪ The Letting Out My Feelings Book ▪ Daily Classroom Journal ▪ storage areas ▪ classroom library ▪ leveling classroom books ▪ Quiet Corner ▪ student seating ▪ word wall ▪ posting rules, consequences, schedules, and learning objectives ▪ bulletin boards

2   Student Organization   26

▪ daily checklists ▪ pencil boxes ▪ work folders ▪ organization of desk and work space ▪ completed-work trays ▪ take-home folders ▪ homework management ▪ weekly jobs/responsibilities ▪ illustrated examples of submitted work

3   Teacher Organization   35

▪ creating a daily routine ▪ intervention strategies ▪ properly scheduling administrative duties ▪ planning lessons in advance

- weekly preparation of materials ▪ documentation
- communicating with parents ▪ preparing for observations

4 Lesson Plans and Units 53

- components of a formal lesson plan ▪ differentiated activities ▪ researching topics ▪ technology ▪ units ▪ rubrics ▪ making adjustments ▪ samples of formal lesson plans ▪ rubric example ▪ unit overview

PART II: Routines, Rules, and Reinforcement

5 Routines 93

- setting schedules ▪ creating simple procedures ▪ modeling simple procedures ▪ examples of procedures ▪ bathroom procedures ▪ consistency

6 Rules 99

- number of rules ▪ positively stating rules ▪ examples of rules ▪ consequences ▪ examples of consequences ▪ engaging students in the discussions about rules and consequences ▪ scenarios

7 Reinforcement 108

- positive reinforcement ▪ negative reinforcement ▪ alternatives to negative reinforcement ▪ ignoring the behavior ▪ physical proximity ▪ redirecting behaviors ▪ separation from the group

PART III: Behavior Management Systems

8 Creating Behavior Management Systems 115

- how to create a behavior system ▪ questions to answer when creating a management system ▪ simplicity ▪ setting attainable goals ▪ setting attainable behavioral objectives ▪ defining classroom rules and consequences ▪ selecting rewards

9 Individual Plans and Group Plans 121

- examples of individual plans ▪ examples of group plans ▪ strategies for children with special needs ▪ "stoplight" ▪ breathing techniques ▪ calming music station

10 The Universal Behavior Plan   130

▪ purpose of the universal behavior plan ▪ how to create a universal behavior plan ▪ communicating with other caregivers ▪ example of a universal behavior plan

Recommended Readings   143

Index   147

About the Author   149

Foreword

This book assists new teachers with suggestions for classroom management, getting acquainted with students, the development of an instructional materials file, and so forth. Effective classroom management leads to a better learning situation, and it should begin the moment students enter the classroom. As the school year begins, spend time getting to know your students. Tell your students about the trials and tribulations you had when you were a student and listen to your students. You, the new teacher, will survive.

Lydia Masao has based this book upon her teaching experiences. Intended to empower beginning teachers and provide strategies to help them survive and thrive in the classroom, this survival guide is dedicated to those who sing, "So little time, so much to do."

Masao has held on to memories from her time as a first-year teacher, and she uses those experiences to guide new teachers through their first year of school. She, like numerous educators, had student teaching experience under the close mentorship of a veteran teacher before being on her own. She shares such pearls from both her veteran mentor's experience and her own experience since that year, noting that beginning teachers need to build good relationships with their students, parents, and colleagues; organize their time efficiently and get past the rough spots; and learn how to manage normal stress and avoid burnout. The first year of teaching is rewarding and challenging, but new teachers must firmly plant their feet on solid ground.

Lucretia Jackson

Introduction

In August 2002, I was embarking on my first year as an elementary school teacher. After going through the county-mandated orientation, I found myself standing in an empty classroom that was my blank canvas. The room presented me with the challenges of creating the environment that would reflect my teaching skills and a warm ambience that provoked learning.

I felt completely overwhelmed with all I had to do in a week's time: decorate and organize the classroom, get books for my students, complete endless administrative duties, plan lessons for at least the first two weeks of school, and on and on. I was on the verge of experiencing a full-fledged meltdown that I hadn't had since I was two.

I pulled myself together, like all first-year teachers, and got to work. I would spend 12+-hour days in my room and still not really put a dent in my ever-growing "to-do" list. In the midst of all this first-year chaos, I learned that one of my students had been labeled a "true behavior problem." I knew then that my first year as a teacher was going to be a baptism by fire into the profession of teaching.

During the course of that year and the subsequent years that followed, I reached the goals I had set for myself when I first walked into my classroom. The keys that allowed me to create the classroom I desired and manage it effectively were organization; the 3 R's of routine, rules, and reinforcement; and an effective behavior management system.

This book outlines clearly the steps in achieving the aforementioned keys and permits first-year as well as veteran teachers to create the structured classrooms they desire. The procedures and plans discussed are not theories but, rather, the successful results of what has been implemented and proven to work in my classroom.

I
ORGANIZATION

1

The Physical Organization of the Classroom

The organization of your classroom is paramount to effective management. There are three areas of organization that should be focused on: physical organization, student organization, and teacher organization.

The physical configuration of your classroom will have an impact on every aspect of the learning process that takes place there. Upon entering your classroom, keep in mind it is your blank canvas. And as is the case for any good artist, it is best to first sketch what you want your final product to look like.

There are certain necessities to every elementary classroom that you should be conscious of when setting up your room. These include:

- centers
- storage areas
- a classroom library
- seating for the children
- a Quiet Corner
- a word wall
- visibly posted rules and consequences
- visibly posted schedules
- visibly posted learning objectives
- bulletin boards

Working with the frame of reference that elementary students build their sight word knowledge through their environment, there should be many signs in your room that assign purpose to each area. On the first day of school, you should give your students a tour of the classroom. Point out the various signs for each area and discuss the rules for each area. I suggest going over this repeatedly the first few weeks of school.

Centers are the place where a large portion of language arts–based activities will take place. Centers should be designed to engage all learners via their individual learning styles. These basic learning styles are visual, auditory, and tactile/kinesthetic.

Visual learners are those who learn best when the subject matter is presented to them through visual tools, such as graphs, charts, reading passages, maps, and pictures. Auditory learners are engaged through the vehicle of sound. These are learners who learn through lectures, music, and any auditory-based lessons.

Tactile/kinesthetic learners are hands-on learners who are cognitively stimulated through movement. In order to learn and master an objective, they must create something or participate in a physical activity that teaches the learning objective. These learners thrive in arts-centered, motions-based, or manipulatives-focused lessons.

Differentiated activities must also be used in centers as well as part of all lesson plans. Daily lessons serve as the springboard for the activities. All of the students are taught the same topic, but the activities they complete at their desks, homes, and centers are based on their level: high, medium, or low.

For instance, if you are teaching a unit on spiders in which the students will have to research a particular type of spider, questions, reading passages, and research tools (such as websites, podcasts, DVDs, and CDs) should be created or selected based on reading and ability level. High-level learners should always have the most challenging work, while middle- and lower-level students should receive assignments that are at or slightly above their levels. Auditory and visual learners will be most engaged through these research activities.

For tactile/kinesthetic learners, you can have each group create a replica of the spider being researched. All reading passages should introduce new vocabulary. Chapter 4, "Lesson Plans and Units," will discuss in depth creating lessons for all learners.

Three centers that will be staples in your elementary classroom are listening, writing, and math centers. Listening centers help build and enforce:

- vocabulary
- sight word knowledge
- listening skills
- phonetic principles

Listening centers should be used in upper elementary grades as a tool to bring below-level readers up to and beyond grade level. All types of learners are given the opportunity to connect letters and words with their correct sounds, pronunciations, spellings, and uses.

The key components of a listening center are:

- a tape player and/or CD player
- several headphones
- folders that will contain the students' assignments for each activity
- manipulatives, such as magnetic letters, numbers, and words
- a small board that assigns the students in each group some of the following jobs:
  - CD/tape player operator
  - materials manager (this person distributes all the materials to everyone in the group)
  - on-task manager
  - organizer (who makes sure the center is left in order)

The listening center should be positioned near the word wall. Teach your students at the beginning of the year to reference the word wall for words they have already learned. Your students will build upon their vocabularies through the activities at the listening center.

Lower-level learners should use the listening center three to four times per week to reinforce high-frequency and sight word knowledge, expand their vocabularies, and increase reading fluency. Mid-level learners should engage in listening center activities twice a week, while high-level learners should use the center once per week.

A wide range of activities can take place at a listening center. Students can listen to text as they follow along in the written text. They can also learn how to successfully execute oral directions by engaging in activities that instruct them to complete specified tasks. More complicated instructions should be given in the upper elementary grades.

Another use for the listening center is to have students listen to phonetics-based activities and complete assignments that reinforce them. For example, primary students learning about the "amp" word family can listen to a lesson that gives examples of words in that family.

As the students listen to the examples, they can be instructed to create the words stated with magnetic letters. The students can then be instructed to create words in the "amp" family that begin with a blend or digraph using the magnetic letters. The listening center is also a great place to have students complete reader response activities after listening to stories. An example of a lesson plan for the listening center is given in Chapter 4.

Writing centers are an integral part of the literacy process. The writing center should also be placed near the listening center, word wall, and classroom library. The center should contain:

- paper
- a picture dictionary (primary grades only)
- a text-based dictionary with illustrations
- text-only dictionaries
- magnetic letters
- a "Letting Out My Feelings"/"Daily Classroom Journal" book
- grammar exercises
- handwriting exercises

THE PHYSICAL ORGANIZATION OF THE CLASSROOM

- illustrated examples of the writing process you want your students to use
- various writing prompts
- examples of well-written stories, paragraphs, or passages
- a publication book that contains all of the students' published works

Two types of dictionaries are suggested for all elementary classrooms to engage all learning levels. In the primary grades, picture only and text with illustrations are recommended. Upper elementary classrooms should have text with illustrations and text-only dictionaries. In each classroom, the former dictionary allows for smooth transition to the latter.

Magnetic letters allow tactile/kinesthetic learners, as well as learners who have difficulty spelling, to take a different, more concrete approach to spelling words correctly during the writing process. Magnetic letters should be utilized in every classroom.

The Letting Out My Feelings Book is something I instituted in my classroom to curtail tattling. The general rule is if someone didn't hit you, yell at you, or take something from you, write down the incident in the book. Students are not allowed to read what someone else wrote, and only one person at a time is allowed to use the book.

This same concept is translated to upper elementary grades with the Daily Classroom Journal. Students in these grades should use the book to chronicle particular events in their day. The journal will consist of each student having their own folders labeled with their names. Each folder will contain writing paper. Model to each student exactly how you want each journal entry to look in regard to date, time, etc. By utilizing these books, students learn to express themselves through text. Students who have a negative reaction to writing will participate easily in writing down their own feelings and thoughts.

Grammar exercises constantly reinforce the many rules of grammar that young writers must remember. By having students complete different exercises, such as daily oral language, their writing skills will improve tremendously. You should also post grammar rules that you are currently working on at the center on sentence strips with examples that support these rules.

Listed below are some examples of basic grammar rules and their supporting examples:

- All sentences start with a capital letter and end with a punctuation mark.
  - Spiders have eight legs.
- Always capitalize names, days of the week, and months in a sentence.
  - On Mondays, we go to Mr. Brown's room to learn about holidays in December.
- Use a period (.) at the end of a telling (declarative) sentence.
  - I have cookies for snack.
- Use a question mark (?) at the end of an asking (interrogatory) sentence.
  - What time is recess?
- Use an exclamation point (!) at the end of an excited (exclamatory) sentence.
  - Watch out for that bus!
- Use a comma when you are listing three or more person, places, or things.
  - She gave me green, yellow, blue, and black crayons.

Handwriting exercises are meant to correct, reinforce, and strengthen handwriting skills. I suggest having students complete handwriting exercises at least once per week, depending on their abilities.

Another major aspect of the writing center is the writing process. There are many examples of steps in the writing process, but the process always includes:

- brainstorming
- writing
- editing
- publishing

Give your students clear examples of each stage in the process and model it consistently to them. As your young writers become more skillful, they should be able to use the writing process independently.

Writing prompts are essential to a successful writing center. With the progress of the school year, your students will become more independent and skilled writers. Always have writing prompts available that are current and correlate to what they are learning at the time.

Writing prompts should be interesting and varied by learning level. You should have your students use the center at least three times per week. Lower-level learners should participate in activities in the center every day.

Many children learn through examples. It is imperative that your students are given examples of well-written passages, paragraphs, and stories at the writing center. These examples should be created by you and the class at the beginning of a new topic or unit.

For instance, if your class is about to start a unit on myths, after reading or listening to a myth, you and the class can write a myth together using the various steps of the writing process. After the final draft has been created, post it at the writing center and have your students reference it as they write about whatever writing prompt you have given them on the topic.

Another integral center in your classroom should be the math center. Your students should engage in activities at the math center daily. Some of these activities should include journaling solutions to various math problems, practicing timed math drills for addition, subtraction, multiplication and/or division problems, solving one-step, two-step, and multi-step word problems daily, etc. The activities at the math center should correlate with what you are currently teaching and constantly reinforce what the students have already learned. Some necessary components of a math center are:

- math journals
- flash cards (addition, subtraction, multiplication, and division)
- money

- base ten set
- calculators
- counters
- pattern blocks
- rulers
- scratch paper
- clocks
- minute math sheets and timer
- whiteboards, markers and erasers
- measuring jars and scales

The word wall is filled with high-frequency words the students will learn weekly. The wall should be located near the writing center, listening center, and classroom library. High-frequency words are words that readers frequently encounter when reading various texts and must know upon sight. These are sometimes called sight words.

The words should be categorized into alphabetical groups. For example, all words beginning with the letter "A" should be placed under a letter "A" on the word wall. As you buy supplies for your classroom before the beginning of the school year, buy alphabet letters to create your word wall. You will constantly be adding words underneath each letter throughout the school year.

Students are usually taught at least five high-frequency words per week that they must be able to spell, read, and use in a sentence correctly by the week's end. At the end of each week, place the words on the word wall and reference previously learned words. This is part of the "word wall ceremony."

In the ceremony, the teacher asks the students to spell the word aloud. The teacher chooses a student to use the word in a sentence, and another student places it on the wall. Always reference the word wall as frequently as possible throughout the school day to reinforce the spelling, meaning, and usage of previously learned words.

There are many fun and effective activities that can be created using the word wall. One activity that I used frequently, especially among my low-level readers, was high-frequency word check. Each student had his or her own set of high-frequency word flash cards. These were 3" × 5" note cards on which students wrote one high-frequency word each as words were introduced.

During their reading time, if students found a sentence that they liked that contained the word, they would write the sentence on the card. Then, during reading group, the students would spread out all of their cards in front of them. I would say a high-frequency word, and the first student to pick up the correct card would raise his or her hand. Then the student would have to read the word, spell it aloud, and read the sentence he or she chose.

The classroom library should be near the writing center and word wall. Books should be categorized or leveled, and this system of organization should be reinforced from day one. Color-coding books by placing a colored sticker on their spines, backs, or covers is one of the simplest ways to organize. Here is an example of an organizing system that you can reformat to fit your classroom:

- Green dots: picture books
- Red dots: picture books that have identifying words, for instance, a picture of the sun with the word *sun* written underneath
- Blue dots: books for early readers with simple sentences such as "The dog is big."
- Yellow dots: books with pictures and complex sentences such as "James ran across the room to meet his mother and father."
- Black dots: simple chapter books such as the Junie B. Jones series and the Frog and Toad series
- Purple dots: more complex chapter books like *Superfudge* by Judy Blume or *The Giver* by Lois Lowry

If you have difficulty, your school's reading specialist, literacy coach, or librarian can help you level the books. When teaching various topics, always check out the books available at your school, city, or county libraries. Don't put stickers on the books. Instead, get bins or baskets that have colored cards on the front that correlate to your system.

Divide the books appropriately into their correct bins. During your reading group time, explain to the students in each group which books you would like them to read according to your system. For example, if you want your highest-level readers to concentrate on reading books within the black or purple range, tell them to get books with these stickers or out of these bins or baskets.

Always encourage your students, no matter their level, to try more challenging books and passages. To prevent them from selecting a book that is too difficult for them, teach them the five-finger rule. To use the five-finger rule, have a student read a page out of a book. At the beginning, his or her hand should be in the position of a fist. For every word the student doesn't know, he or she must raise a finger. By the end of the page, if the student has all five fingers out of the fisted position, the book is too difficult. If the student still has one or more fingers in the fisted position, he or she can read the book.

The Quiet Corner is one of my favorite tools to use in a classroom. In the current world of high-stakes testing, the workloads are intensifying. If adults need a break or two in the course of their workday, so do children. The Quiet Corner is designed specifically for this purpose. The Quiet Corner should be an inviting, comfortable place. My Quiet Corner consisted of:

- a large, comfortable chair
- a silent timer
- the Quiet Corner rules
- a basket of books

At the beginning of the school year, explain clearly to the children the purpose of the Quiet Corner. Explain to the students that the Quiet Corner is a place they can go when they need a break. Students should use the Quiet Corner for 10 minutes each time they are there. Limit the use of the Quiet Corner to twice a day.

Be explicit when presenting the ground rules for the use of the Quiet Corner. Here are some examples of rules to enforce:

- As soon as you enter the Quiet Corner, set the timer for ten (10) minutes.
- You may read one of the books in the basket or bring your own.
- You can use the Quiet Corner only twice a day.
- One person at a time is allowed in the Quiet Corner.
- The Quiet Corner must be quiet at all times.

The Quiet Corner should be set up in a quiet place in your classroom, away from the other centers. Placing it near your desk is always a good option that allows you to monitor the area more effectively and allows the children to be closer to you, which they love.

The first day of the school year can be overwhelming. Not only do you have to go over the rules, help the children adjust to their new environment, teach as much as possible, and complete various administrative duties, but you also have to deal with the massive amount of supplies that are brought in by the students for the school year.

On the first day of school, I would collect all of the supplies. I had shelves and cubbyholes in my room that I used to store the supplies. You may not have this in your room, but you can easily purchase and use baskets to store supplies. Designate an area for pencils, erasers, scissors, glue, crayons, paint, paintbrushes, snacks, smocks and t-shirts, all-purpose spray cleaner, other cleaning supplies, etc. Clearly label each area.

At the end of each day, have the teacher's assistant place your supplies in the correct area to keep your room looking orderly. Always remember that as an elementary teacher, your entire room should always promote literacy. This happens when every area is clearly labeled. This facilitates not only reading but organization as well.

Depending on your school district, you should be allotted a certain amount of money to order supplies. These supplies will be used to fill the supply baskets initially for each row and then each table or group. A comprehensive shopping list is provided at the end of this chapter.

You don't have to purchase every item on the list. If you are a new teacher, you will probably inherit some of the items on the list from the previous teacher. There will also be items on the list that can be placed on the student supply list.

Along with a storage area for classroom supplies, there should be an area clearly designated for the children's book bags and coats. If you have a closet with hooks, assign each child a hook to place their belongings by writing their names underneath their hooks. Your classroom may not have a closet, so cubbies are the next best thing. Label each cubby with the students' names.

One of the most important areas to organize in your classroom is your students' desks. At the beginning of every school year, it is best to arrange the desks in rows. If your class roster consists of 25 children, I recommend creating five rows of five desks.

Divide the rows as evenly as possible, and ensure that each desk faces the front of the room, where your chalkboard or whiteboard is located. Place a name tag on each desk. In the early primary grades (K–1), name tags with a number line, the primary colors, and the alphabet written in manuscript are most helpful. In the upper grades, simple name tags will suffice.

Many teachers like to assign students' desks in alphabetical order; however, I prefer to assign students' desks by gender. I tended to have more boys than girls in my classroom each school year, and arrangement by gender helped ensure that each row had a good mix of girls and boys. Be as creative as possible when assigning seats so that dispersion of students is ideal.

Rows are to be used at the beginning of the year to establish routine and set the pace and expectations of the class. When desks are arranged in rows, teachers have time to see which students work best together, determine which students should not be seated near one another, and slowly introduce group seating.

Group seating promotes cooperative learning, which is very important to the learning process and fostering the classroom dynamic of community. Even though the students are seated individually in rows, the group dynamic can be introduced.

Assign each row a basket of supplies and a weekly row captain. The weekly row captain can be given a laminated star that says "Captain" that can be affixed to his or her desk with VELCRO®. The supply basket will contain a bag of scissors for each person in the row, individual bags of crayons for each student, a bag of markers with enough markers in each color for each student, and bags of colored pencils for each student.

One of the most trying times during the school year will be during the flu and cold season. To curtail the rampant spread of colds, the flu, or sniffles, supply each row or table a box of baby wipes or hand wipes. Instruct students to wipe their hands with a wipe after they sneeze or cough. This made a tremendous difference in cutting down colds in my class.

One of the duties of the row captain is to distribute supplies to the students in their rows as instructed. As the year progresses, the job of row captain will be changed to table captain when the students' desks are arranged to form tables.

Once you get a feel for which students should be placed together, enhance the group dynamic in the classroom by reconfiguring the students' desks to form tables. To further foster the concept of cooperative learning and working together in a group, have each table come up with a group name. Let the students know that the names will remain for each table throughout the school year, but students can be moved to other tables.

I have created a behavior system that is conducive to this seating arrangement and is explained in further detail in Chapter 9, "Individual Plans and Group Plans." Each group should have the same number of students, though a group may have one student fewer or more than the others. Within each group, try to partner students in a high-level learner to low-level learner pattern.

When configuring students' desks, allow space for movement. During my third year of teaching, my new principal wanted to see more movement in each classroom. She based this requirement on studies that found movement stimulates learning, especially in primary grades. I arranged my students' desk in a design that permitted them to move easily and freely during morning exercises.

Morning exercises lasted about 5 minutes and got the creative juices flowing for the day. The exercises generally consisted of sets of jumping jacks, frog hops, and stretches. This allowance for space was also used when the students partnered to work on the floor.

An important note is that your classroom should be designed to evoke a comfortable, homelike atmosphere that stimulates learning. It should be a place that is inviting and draws children in. Creating the proper setting is almost like decorating your home but with the goal of creating a community atmosphere that is safe, fun, and challenging. I have taught children who have felt safer in the classroom than they did in their own homes, and that leaves a lasting, positive effect that is priceless.

The front of your classroom where your chalkboard or whiteboard is located will be its focal point. This is where you should post your classroom rules (always stated positively), consequences, daily schedule, specials schedule, and daily and quarterly learning objectives. The rules of your classroom should be placed side by side with the consequences of not following the rules. Forming rules and consequences and how they should be stated and presented to the children is discussed in further detail in Chapter 6, "Rules."

Your daily schedule and specials schedule should be placed next to one another. The number of your students who actually refer to these schedules will be surprising. Daily learning objectives should be changed frequently as objectives are taught. These should be written on your whiteboard or chalkboard. Your quarterly learning objectives should be written on sentence strips.

Divide the learning objectives into subject matter areas. The daily objectives that correlate to a particular quarterly objective should be written underneath them. See Figure 1.1 for an example.

At the beginning of each quarter, discuss the quarterly objectives with the students. In the mornings, as you go over your daily schedule, discuss each daily objective. This allows students, parents, and administrators to see how each objective will be accomplished.

I suggest not only writing your quarterly objectives on sentence strips but also laminating them. This will permit frequent use until objectives are revised. Your school district should provide a pacing guide that advises when objectives should be taught. Use this guide as your springboard when you meet with your grade level to plan weekly lessons and activities.

Language Arts:
I am learning to use the dictionary to spell and define words. (Quarterly Objective)

I will use the dictionary to find out what the words *desert*, *rainforest*, and *plains* mean. (Daily Objective)

Math:
I am learning to add single digits. (Quarterly Objective)

I will use my addition facts to complete my additional wheel for +2. (Daily Objective)

Social Studies:
I am learning about my immediate community. (Quarterly Objective)

I will make a map of my street. (Daily Objective)

Science:
I am learning the four seasons and their differences. (Quarterly Objective)

I will complete my "Apple Tree in Four Seasons" book. (Daily Objective)

FIGURE 1.1

Bulletin boards are a necessity in every elementary classroom. Every class should have the following bulletin boards:

- a display of students' work
- a bulletin board correlating to specific subject matter the students are learning about
- a job board
- a character-building board

A display of students' work helps instill a sense of pride in a job well done and promotes a good work ethic. My display board was placed next to the word wall and could be seen prominently in the room.

Bulletin boards that are based on subject matter being taught should be changed frequently. I suggest using long-term units for this board to lessen your workload. One of the best ways to maximize your subject matter board is to make it interactive. For instance, you can place on the board fun trivia questions about the subject for students to answer.

Job boards designate students' specific duties within the classroom. These jobs should be changed weekly. Some examples of jobs to have in your classroom are:

- teacher's assistant
- girls' restroom monitor
- boys' restroom monitor
- line leader
- caboose
- messenger
- mail clerk
- homework/paper collector
- paper distributor

There are many other jobs that can be created for the children in your classroom. I advise creating jobs that are specific to your room and help the flow of the day.

Most school districts have a character-building program that helps instill different attributes, such as responsibility, honesty, and kindness. The program in my district was called "Character Counts." Your bulletin board should name the different characteristics and give examples.

You can also make the character-building board an interactive board in which the students can write examples of the different characteristics being displayed by other students in the class. You might create an award that can be provided to students when their classmates observe them displaying a given characteristic and how it was done. A reproducible chart is given at the end of this chapter; Figure 1.2 provides an example of recognizing honesty.

In this chapter we discussed the basic setup of an organized classroom. Some of the essential components are centers and their diverse uses, storage areas, a classroom library, and bulletin boards. A classroom that has good physical organization relies on proper placement, arrangement, and labeling of each area. The various uses of each area are clearly defined and modeled at the beginning of the school year. All of these elements are important in maintaining a classroom beneficial to learning.

See Quick Tips for ideas on organizing your classroom and Figure 1.3 for an example of good classroom design.

CONGRATULATIONS

Olivia García showed honesty when she turned in the wallet she found in the office.

That was honest! Presented by: Ms. Masao on September 15, 2008.

FIGURE 1.2

> **QUICK TIPS**
>
> - Change the arrangement of students' desks at least once or twice per grading period.
> - Be innovative when rearranging students' desks. For instance, arranging desks in the shape of letters is fun and innovative.
> - Less is more. When you decorate your classroom, try not to go overboard.
> - Keep things simple but appealing by decorating with primary colors.

SHOPPING LIST
- Student Supplies
  - for kindergarten students: boxes of beginner's pencils with erasers
  - boxes of unsharpened #2 pencils
  - square erasers
  - for upper elementary students: red, black, blue, and green pens to use in the writing process or diagramming sentences
  - large glue sticks
  - small pair of scissors for each student, plus five more pairs for other students who may enroll as the year progresses
  - steno pads to record homework assignments (grades 2–6)
  - smocks
  - clipboards
- Teacher's Supplies
  - at least two permanent markers
  - highlighters

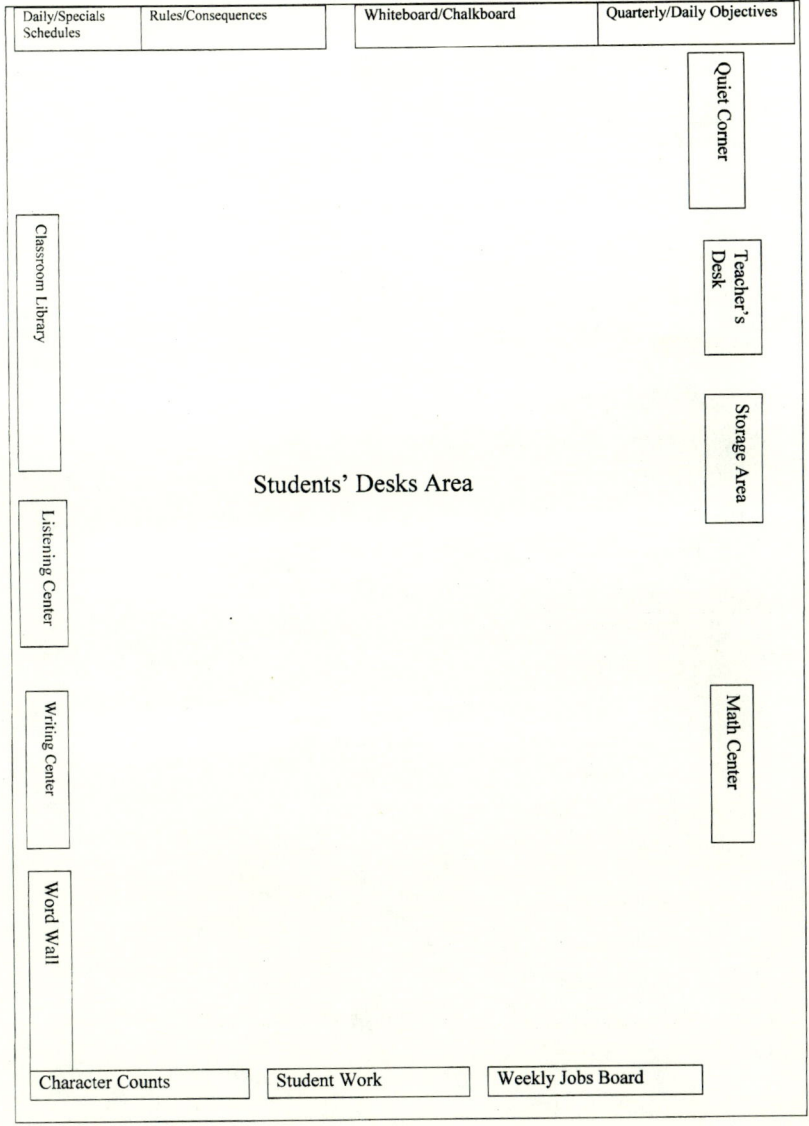

FIGURE 1.3
Example of Good Classroom Design

- a heavy-duty three-hole puncher
- book tape
- push pins
- tape dispenser
- invisible tape refills
- paper clips
- binder clips
- rubber bands
- three boxes of colored file folders
- at least two staplers
- staples
- stickers
- at least seven stackable letter trays
- EZ grader
- plan book
- grade book
- journal to document daily incidents
- sentence strips
- sentence strip organizer to file and store sentence strips
- borders for bulletin boards
- uppercase and lowercase letter packs for bulletin boards
- rubber stamps
- rubber stamp ink pad
- certificates

△ Classroom Supplies
- two pencil boxes of different colors
- electric pencil sharpener
- two dry erase boards for reading groups and center activities
- dry erase pens
- dry erasers
- chalk
- erasers for the classroom chalkboard

THE PHYSICAL ORGANIZATION OF THE CLASSROOM

- for primary grades: 9" × 12" chalkboards for each student; these are often sold in packs of 10
- small erasers for student chalkboards
- mailbox system with enough slots for each child (sometimes called Classroom Keepers® mailbox or bankers box)
- several boxes of large and small plastic storage bags
- VELCRO® (to affix table captain badges on name plates)
- cardstock
- chart tablets (manuscript or cursive, depending on grade level)
- chart stands
- pocket charts
- construction paper
- class pack crayons
- class pack markers
- class pack colored pencils
- disposable containers for the paint
- assorted paint in quart size
- assorted paint brushes
- paint brush stand
- puzzles (for indoor recess)
- card games (for indoor recess)
- board games (for indoor recess)
- first aid kits
- classroom calendar
- name plates

△ Math Supplies
  - rulers for each student
  - magnetic numbers
  - number line 1–100 (primary grades)
  - counters
  - base-10 block sets
  - math activities for the math center

- math flash cards (addition, subtraction, multiplication, and division)
- money kit
- large Judy Clock (primary grades)
- small clocks for each student
- measuring jars

△ Language Arts Supplies
- for primary grades: ruled primary paper
- for upper elementary grades: composition paper (not college ruled)
- magnetic letters
- phonics kits
- high-frequency word tiles
- word-building puzzles (primary grades)
- language arts games
- language arts activities for the listening center

△ Social Studies Supplies
- globe
- states and capitals puzzles
- map skills activities
- wall maps
- history time lines

△ Science Supplies
- greenhouse
- seeds
- magnifying glasses
- body models (heart, teeth, muscles, etc.)
- thermometer
- measuring jars
- magnets
- balances

CONGRATULATIONS

_____

showed _____

when _____

_____

_____.

That was _____!

Presented by _____

on _____.

Character Bulletin Board

2

Student Organization

The learning process can flow more smoothly if your students learn how to organize themselves effectively and you set expectations clearly. Students in the primary grades are very literal, so when teaching them organization skills, you must be as detailed as possible. Successful student organizers in my own classroom are:

- daily checklists
- pencil boxes
- work folders
- organization of desk/work space
- completed-work trays
- take-home folders
- homework management
- weekly jobs and responsibilities
- illustrated examples of how submitted work should look

Each day prepare a checklist of the activities that your students will be expected to complete throughout the day. The checklist should include the students' names and date (e.g., 11/12/07), and it should be arranged in sequential order by subject. For instance, if your language arts block is in the morning, the activities you have planned for them should be listed after morning work.

The activities for the next subject to be covered in your daily schedule should be listed after the language arts activities. Before teaching each day, review the daily checklist. You can have students read each activity aloud. Teach the students to check off completed activities on the list immediately after finishing them.

A great way to ensure that your students use the daily checklist effectively is to create a large checklist on the chalkboard or whiteboard. When you prepare for the first weeks of school, create a large daily checklist for at least the first three weeks. Provide your students with copies of the daily checklist.

Begin the school year by properly modeling how to use the checklist. Instruct your students to check off the completed activities on their copies as you check them off on the large classroom copy. Allow your students the opportunity to complete the activities in each category in any order they want. While you model to the students proper usage of the checklist, also model to them the type of work you would like submitted.

Everything in your classroom should promote the literacy process. The checklist aids students in the reading process, especially when you go over the checklist in the morning. The checklist should be small, so it can fit in the right corner of their desks. Teach the students to always place the checklists there.

It is best to create the checklists as you prepare for the following week. This will allow you time at the end of each day, as you do your daily cleanup, to put the checklists on their desks along with their morning work. This will be part of your routine that will be discussed further in Chapter 3, "Teacher Organization."

Sometimes the students will not be able to finish an assignment in one day. On Tuesdays through Fridays, always list an "unfinished work" category for each subject matter. Figure 2.1 provides an example of a daily checklist given on a Monday.

> Lydia Masao   11/12/07
>
> ### DAILY CHECKLIST
> ____ Morning Work
>
> **Language Arts:**
> ____ Persuasive Paragraph
> ____ Literature Questions
> ____ Listening Center
> ____ Reading Group
>
> **Math:**
> ____ Multiplication Quiz
> ____ Word Problem Relay
>
> **Social Studies:**
> ____ Goods and Services
>
> **Science:**
> ____ Adaptation Book

FIGURE 2.1.
Example of a Daily Checklist

One of my favorite student organizers is the pencil box. The two pencil boxes listed on the shopping list in Chapter 1 are used for this purpose. Label one of the boxes "Pencils" and the other "To Be Sharpened." Each day when the students enter the classroom, they should put away their things and get a pencil out of the "Pencils" box.

You should order these pencils, along with an electric pencil sharpener and erasers, if your school district provides money to order supplies. If your school system does not provide such money, school supply catalogs generally offer these items cheaply.

If a pencil tip breaks or becomes dull, the student should place it in the "To Be Sharpened" box and get another pencil from the "Pencil" box. This eliminates time often wasted when students get up to sharpen their pencils and keeps them focused on whatever task they are trying to complete. Each week select one student to be the pencil sharpener.

The pencil sharpener should sharpen the pencils in the "To Be Sharpened" box before the class leaves for lunch and at the end of the day. While your students clean up and prepare for lunch, the sharpener should be sharpening the pencils. By incorporating the "Pencils" and "To Be Sharpened" boxes in your class, you will eliminate arguments over pencils, maximize instructional time, reduce dead time in which students are not engaged in learning, and prevent opportunities for mischief.

As a rule of thumb, sharpen at least three pencils per student to ensure that the "Pencils" box always has an adequate supply of pencils, and distribute one square eraser to each student at the beginning of the year. Explain to the students that they are responsible for their own erasers.

Work folders are used for students to deposit their uncompleted work. Some of the colored folders listed on the shopping list will be used as the students' work folders. Label each student's folder with his or her name. When introducing the daily routine, teach your students to keep the folders on the left sides of their desks and place uncompleted work in them.

Explain that if students have any free time, they should work on uncompleted work in their folders for that particular subject. For instance, if a student completes all of his or her language arts activities before the language arts block is complete, he or she should pull out any previously unfinished language arts work to complete. Students should not work on lessons in subjects other than that being studied in a given block: for example, students should not work on unfinished math during the language arts block. This will be discussed further in Chapter 5, "Routines."

Students should keep the work in their work folders as neat as possible. You should show them examples of neat work folders and reward them for maintaining this neatness. Your students can use paper clips to keep uncompleted work attached by subject matter.

As a warning, K–1 students will have difficulty manipulating paper clips correctly. Teach these students to keep all subject matter work piled together and all work folders on the left sides of their desks.

Your students' space should be as organized as possible. If it is cluttered and messy, they cannot give their best. Teach your students from day one where everything should be placed on and in their desks. Remember that elementary students don't know how to organize themselves, but you do.

Teach your students how the interior of their desks should look. I suggest placing large books on the bottom and smaller books on top to keep the desks neat. Nameplates should be on desktops, daily checklists should be in the upper right-hand corner, and folders should be on the left side of the desks.

A master special education teacher at my school advised me to have students place their pencils on their nameplates when they were not using them. Keeping their pencils on their desks prevented the pencils from entering the great abyss that desks can sometimes become. This also became a great routine that eliminated pencil loss in the classroom.

I did frequent desk checks to positively reinforce the skill of maintaining a neat desk. I would suddenly announce "desk check," and the students with the neatest desks would receive a prize.

You can teach your students to check their own desks and the desks of their row/table mates. When you promote more cooperative learning, checking and rewarding neat desks by rows/tables will enforce the group dynamic. The chief responsibility for ensuring that all desks are neat in a particular row or table belongs to the desk checker.

Students should place all completed work in the correct completed-work tray. Completed-work trays are stackable trays that can be bought inexpensively at office supply stores or when placing your supply orders through your school system. These trays were also included on the shopping list in Chapter 1.

Assign each row or table a tray labeled with the row/table name. Explain to the students that once they complete an assignment, they should place it in their assigned tray. The trays can be placed in the front of the room or in an area close to your desk. At the end of the day, the collector should collect all of the completed assignments in the trays and neatly place them in the "To Be Graded" tray on your desk.

Take-home folders should be given to each student. Some school districts supply weekly take-home folders. The folders are to be taken home on a particular day every week and returned the following day with parents' signatures. The folder should house:

- graded work
- correspondence to parents
- your weekly, monthly, or quarterly newsletter
- homework, if it is assigned on a weekly basis
- permission slips
- school newsletter
- student averages in each subject every two weeks
- any other pertinent information

The take-home folders should be kept at the mail center when not in use. The folders should have an area where parents can sign, date, and write any comments or concerns. It is imperative to stress the importance of returning the signed folders in a timely manner to parents as an effective means of communication. Take-home folders should be discussed during Back-to-School Night.

In the early primary grades (K–1), I suggest students be given homework assignments on a weekly basis. These homework assignments should be distributed on Mondays and collected on Fridays. Homework assignments for K–1 students should include a calendar, detailing what should be completed daily.

For students in grades 2 through 6, homework assignments should be recorded by the students daily in a homework pad. Steno pads are best for homework pads and were included on the shopping list in Chapter 1. You should model to the students how the assignments should be written in the pad by providing them with an example at the front of the class.

Ensure daily that the students have properly written down the assignments by having the homework manager check each steno pad before dismissal. Homework policies will be discussed in further detail in Chapter 3, "Teacher Organization."

Student jobs and responsibilities were discussed briefly in Chapter 1. Depending on the number of students in your class, each student should be assigned a job at the beginning of the week. The assignment should last the duration of the week, and jobs should be changed weekly.

At the beginning of the year, when introducing the classroom routines and procedures, discuss the function and expectation of each job. These jobs should be part of a permanent bulletin board. Many teacher's supply stores and school supply catalogs have ready-made bulletin boards for this purpose. Jobs to incorporate on your jobs board and their functions include:

- *Line Leader:* This person is the first in line whenever the class goes somewhere.
- *Caboose:* This person is the last in line and ensures that when the class leaves the room, the door is closed and everyone is in line.
- *Mail Clerk:* This person places graded papers and informational materials given by the front office in each student's mailbox. The day that weekly take-home folders are sent home, the mail clerk should place each student's mail in his or her folder.
- *Pencil Sharpener:* This person sharpens the pencils in the "To Be Sharpened" box twice a day, before lunch and at the end of the day.
- *Collector:* This person should collect all notes, permission slips, pencils, completed work from the trays, take-home folders, and anything else that needs to be collected from the students.
- *Girl's Restroom Monitor:* This girl ensures that when the girls are in the restroom, no one is playing.
- *Boy's Restroom Monitor:* This boy ensures that when the boys are in the restroom, no one is playing.

- *Teacher's Assistant:* This student assists in miscellaneous tasks you need done.
- *Paper Distributor:* This person passes out any papers you want to give your students.
- *Desk Checker:* This person ensures that everyone's desk in his or her row/table is neat. This includes the work folders, desktops, and interiors of the desks.
- *Messenger:* This student runs errands to the front office or to other teachers.
- *Homework Manager:* This student ensures that everyone at his or her row/table has properly written down the daily homework assignment.

Your students will not know the type of work you expect them to submit unless you provide them with clear examples. At the beginning of the school year, instruct your students how to label their papers with their names, date, and subject. An example should be placed at the front of the classroom, in plain sight of everyone.

When your students are creating something, whether it is a book, spider, or any other project, make your own example as a guide. You should also provide students with a rubric for their project. Rubrics, which are discussed further in Chapter 4, will teach your students how to submit neat, well-done work.

In this chapter, we discussed various student organizers and strategies. These included daily checklists, organization of student space, classroom jobs, and homework management. Student organizers are imperative in teaching students effective study habits. These organizers are purposefully regimented, but there is always room for fun.

The purpose of these measures is to set high expectations, produce good work ethics, keep students engaged, and reduce opportunities they may have to get off track. An ultimate reward of using these measures is that they set the parameters necessary to effectively use cooperative learning in the classroom, which is a large part of creating the desired community dynamic.

QUICK TIPS

- Reinforcement, reinforcement, reinforcement! Student organizers can be properly implemented only with constant reinforcement.
- Be consistent when reinforcing the use of the organizers.
- Constant verbal praise and rewards are most beneficial in ensuring that your students will use the organizers properly and effectively.

3

Teacher Organization

Teaching is a demanding profession, no matter the grade level. If you organize yourself effectively, you will improve your performance as a teacher. Your effective organization will include:

- creating a daily routine
- properly scheduling your administrative duties
- planning lessons in advance
- maintaining a concise lesson plan book
- neatly organizing your desk and personal space
- always being prepared for observations
- attending teacher development opportunities
- weekly preparation of materials
- defined homework, make-up work, and grading policies
- concise substitute plans
- documentation
- communicating effectively with parents
- setting succinct guidelines for parent volunteers

Before the year begins, make a list of the tasks that you will need to complete daily. You should decide in advance whether you want to complete these administrative duties early each morning before school starts or after school each day. I suggest completing them at the end of the day.

The more practiced you become in completing each task, the less time it will take to complete. You should plan to set aside approximately an hour to an hour and a half to complete them. Some of these tasks are:

- grading papers each day
- entering the grades in your grade book
- setting out materials for the next day
- changing daily objectives
- filing paperwork
- writing any incidents in your daily journal
- writing about student performance in the student progress file
- answering e-mails or phone calls from parents

Beginning with the first day of school, you should start establishing a routine to complete your daily tasks. To ensure that all of these responsibilities are fulfilled, create a daily checklist that includes your daily routine and any additional duties that need to be finished. Stick to your routine as much as possible.

As discussed in Chapter 2, each day the collector will collect all of the work in the completed-work trays and place them in your "To Be Graded" tray. I recommend using the EZ grader listed on the shopping list to guarantee papers are graded accurately. The assignments, quizzes, or tests your students complete should be graded on a daily basis.

You may be tempted to postpone grading papers until a later date. Speaking from past experience, this is a bad precedent to set. I found that when I delayed grading student work, my end-of-the-quarter tasks were nearly insurmountable, not to mention highly stressful. By keeping your grading up to date, you will also prevent being bogged down with ungraded papers and extra work.

After you have graded the papers, enter them into your grade book. Some school systems have electronic grade books that tabulate and store student averages. I used an electronic grade book but also saved a copy on a flash drive as well as maintained a hard copy. The papers should then be placed in the mail center basket for the mail clerk to file daily.

You should check your students' averages in each subject every two weeks. By doing this, you can pinpoint early any areas of difficulty in mastering particular learning objectives. You will also be able to identify how your students learn best in a particular subject.

When you find an area that needs improvement, several intervention strategies can improve student performance, such as:

- tutoring
- engaging the resources of your school math or reading specialists
- setting aside time in the day for one-on-one help for the student with yourself, a classroom volunteer, or a subject specialist, such as the reading or math specialist
- sending home additional assignments for the student to complete with his or her parents or caregivers

You should become familiar with the various resources the staffs at your school and school district offer to help improve student performance. If your student continues to struggle after all of these intervention strategies have been exhausted, contact your school's guidance counselor about the steps you need to take to have the student evaluated for any possible learning disabilities.

Another important part of your daily routine will be to set out materials for the next day's lessons. This will include morning work, daily checklists, tests, quizzes, etc. These materials will be created weekly. While you distribute these materials, change the daily objectives and date on the front board of your classroom and file any paperwork you may have.

You should have a file folder for each subject, labeled with the name of the subject, including:

- Math Lessons
- Word Wall Lessons
- Social Studies Lessons
- Science Lessons
- Reading Group Lessons (there should be a folder for each level)
- Writing Center Lessons
- Listening Center Lessons
- Math Center Lessons
- Language Arts Lessons

Place the originals for these lessons in the appropriate folders. Place a Post-it® on each original with the date and learning objective of the lesson.

If you continue to teach the same grade, you will reference these files when creating lesson plans. The most strenuous year you will have as a teacher will be your first year. By your second year of teaching, these files will help you in your daily planning and serve as a springboard for other lessons you will create.

In the course of your day, there may be problematic incidents in the classroom. These incidents can range from a case of something stolen to an argument between students to complaints from a specials teacher about the behavior of students. Write these incidents on a Post-it® pad that you should keep with you at all times.

Make sure to note the date, time, and nature of the incident. At the end of the day, write all of these incidents in your daily journal, which will provide documentation. The daily journal was included on the shopping list in chapter 1. A parent or the principal may later reference an incident that has occurred and ask for further explanation. The journal will enable you to accurately relay what happened and any actions you may have taken.

TEACHER ORGANIZATION   39

Student daily performance forms should also be part of your daily documentation routine. This will be discussed in greater detail later in this chapter.

The last part of your daily routine should be responding to any e-mails or phone messages your students' parents send you. At the beginning of the year, clearly communicate to parents the best way to contact you and when you will be able to respond to them daily. My personal preference was e-mail. I never knew when I had voice mail messages because my phone was behind the TV. I made very clear to my parents on Back-to-School Night not to leave me voice mail but, rather, to contact me via e-mail.

Whatever form of communication you choose, give the times that you will be most easily accessible to parents and when they may expect a response to their questions, and stick to these times! Be consistent in replying promptly to any questions or concerns parents may have, or a minor problem or issue can, and often will, turn into a major one.

Depending on your school system and principal, you should be provided with an academic calendar at the beginning of each year. The calendar should include the dates of:

- teacher work days
- parent–teacher conferences
- expected completion of report cards
- testing
- staff meetings
- PTA meetings
- various breaks

Buy a calendar (desk or daily planner), insert these dates, and plan accordingly. When creating your daily checklists, always reference this calendar. If you have paperwork that needs to be completed and submitted on a certain date, plan to have it completed at least one week prior to the due date. This will give you the opportunity to make any revisions necessary before submission.

Your school system should also provide you with a pacing guide of the curriculum. The pacing guide details when and which specific topics should be taught during the school year. These topics should be listed as learning objectives. Try to stay within the time and subject parameters set by the pacing guide. This, along with your grade-level team, will serve as the launch pad of your lesson planning.

I recommend planning monthly or every two weeks. Do *not* plan each day as you enter your classroom! That method of teaching will render you ineffective as a teacher. You should select one day each month to plan for the entire month or one day every two weeks to plan biweekly. Write this date in your calendar and adhere to it. When creating your lesson plans, be inclusive of all learning styles.

As you plan, keep all lessons in your lesson plan book, which your principal may provide or which you can purchase at your local teacher's supply store. Always ensure that your lesson plan book is current and detailed. The objectives, materials, simply stated procedures, assignments, and assessments should be listed for each lesson. You do not need to go into great detail, but your principal should be able to read the plans and know what your students will be doing.

I advise always keeping your lesson plan book open on your desk, so it is easily accessible to your principal or other administrative staff members for unannounced observations. Your desk should be neat and well organized. This will serve as an example to your students and an effective way to keep you organized.

On your desk you should have your

- calendar
- lesson plan book
- grade book
- "To Be Graded" tray
- materials for the week's lessons
- any other necessary materials

During my first year of teaching, I struggled to keep my desk neat, and my principal pointed this out to me. A disorganized work area needlessly increased my workload. I learned to get into the habit of cleaning up my work area during the day.

The logic of the old saying "Live each day like it's your last" should also apply to your classroom. Enter your classroom each day with the expectation of being observed. Your principal is required to observe your performance as a teacher a prescribed number of times per school year. He or she will be looking for all or some of the following:

- You are teaching the required objectives within the timeframe required by your school system.
- Classroom rules and current objectives are clearly and visibly stated in child-friendly language.
- Differentiated activities exist that engage all learning styles.
- Good teacher organization exists.
- Good student organization exists.
- Well-maintained and current grade and lesson plan books are easily accessible to the principal.
- An effective behavior management system is in use.
- There is plenty of positive reinforcement to students.
- A well-organized and neatly maintained classroom that promotes learning exists.
- You are clearly in charge of your classroom, and learning is being easily and successfully facilitated.

By following your daily routine, staying organized, and effectively using your behavior management system, you will ensure a good observation. Before the school year begins, sit down with your principal and ask exactly what expectations he or she has for your classroom, especially during observations. Make a list of these expectations and incorporate them in your daily routine and planning.

Your grade-level chair will be another excellent resource in explaining what is expected of you. Part of the chair's job is to ensure that each teacher on the team is meeting the school system's and principal's expectations. Given the opportunity, ask your principal if you can observe any teachers at your school who exemplify exactly what he or she is looking for.

Once your principal has conducted an observation, discuss it with him or her. During the discussion, your principal should touch on your strengths and areas that need improvement. You should be proactive in this process by respectfully asking your principal for recommendations of how to improve these areas.

Get a copy of the observation and let it serve as a compass in selecting teacher development activities. A good teacher is always learning. Teacher development is essential in becoming a master teacher.

The best teachers I know are always the ones who want to learn more about their craft. Undoubtedly, your school will require you to attend a certain number of teacher development activities. You should attend these as well as others that will improve your teaching and classroom management.

Your school system's website should list opportunities and websites for teaching programs at local colleges, universities, and libraries. There may also be educator programs at local museums. Put all of these resources to use, especially in the summer.

At the end of the school year, go through your observations and target two or three areas you want to improve upon during the summer. You should select books as well as workshops that concentrate on these areas. Your school system should employ subject matter experts at its headquarters. Contact these experts and ask them to recommend books or activities you can participate in.

As discussed earlier in this chapter, part of your daily routine will include distributing materials for the next day's lessons. The materials that you will need to execute the plans should be prepared in advance. All materials should be created, gathered, or copied on a weekly basis.

For instance, checking out books, creating the students' daily checklists, and making photocopies for the following week can be done every Friday and will reduce the time you have to stay after school. Label folders by subject matter and place the materials in the correlating subject folders. These folders will be different from the lessons folders mentioned earlier (e.g., "Social Studies Materials").

Homework, make-up work, and grading policies should be clearly defined and explained to your students and their parents from the start. Your school district and principal will already have these policies in place, and you will be expected to adhere to them. If you do not understand the policies, ask your grade-level chair or principal (preferably in that order) to clarify them.

After you get a clear understanding of the policies, write them in child-friendly language and post them very visibly in your classroom. When you meet with parents for the first time, give them written copies of the policies. Be concise when explaining the policies to both parents and students.

If your school district or principal gives you general guidelines for these policies, create specific policies for your classroom. For instance, ensure that your students and parents know what percentage of grades homework will be. If a student turns in homework late, clearly state in your policy whether he or she will be given a grace period or how many points will be deducted for tardiness.

Some school districts limit the amount of homework that may be given to students. For example, my school district required that students in the primary grades should do no more than 30 minutes of homework per night. Your homework should reflect any requirements your school district and principal have. Remember that homework is meant to reinforce and review skills that have already been taught. If you have a class website, ensure weekly or daily homework is listed on it.

In regards to make-up work, create a folder containing copies of make-up work that students can access when they return to school. This folder must be kept current with your weekly lesson plans. Let your students know how much time they have to complete the make-up work. Do not overwhelm students with make-up work. Ensure that the make-up work reviews the fundamentals of what they missed during their absence. If you have a class website, upload these materials for students who have Internet access at home.

Your grading policy should also be in alignment with what your school district and principal require. Give each student a laminated copy of the grading policy that accurately reflects the value of grades A, B, C, D, and F. For instance, an A in your school district may be 93–100 percent or 90–100 percent. These copies should be affixed to their work folders. In the primary grades, teachers sometimes use:

- E for excellent, which is equivalent to an A
- G for good, which is equivalent to a B
- S for satisfactory, which is equivalent to a C
- N for needs improvement, which is equivalent to a D
- U for unsatisfactory, which is equivalent to an F

Rubrics, discussed in Chapter 4, should also be part of your grading policy when grading projects.

There will be days when you just won't be able to go to school. To ensure that your students are still learning, create very detailed substitute plans that include any requirement your principal may have. At the beginning of the year, give your sub plan folder to your grade-level chair or principal for review. Good sub plans will have:

- a letter to your substitute (an example is given at the end of this chapter)
- a detailed schedule of the daily events
- a seating chart
- copies, already made, of work your students should complete
- a to-do list of anything you want your sub to do before you return
- the names of teachers your sub can contact for help
- the names of responsible students in the class who can answer any routine classroom questions
- fire drill and evacuation procedures
- any special instructions for children who take medication or have allergies

In a school system, there will always be great subs who will do an amazing job as well as subs who will leave your kids with nightmarish stories. To help prevent getting the latter type of substitute, ask your grade-level chair, various teachers in your school, and your principal to provide the names and numbers of good subs. Make a contact list for all of these subs and keep them at home to contact when you are absent.

You should also inform a team member or your grade-level chair that you will be absent. One of my students did not deal well with my absences and made the day difficult for a sub. As a counteractive measure, I made prior arrangements to have him go to my teammate's classroom for the day. You may also have a student for whom you will have to make this type of prior arrangement. Make sure the student knows whose class to go to and that your sub and principal know the situation. Follow any procedures already in place for reporting your absence. If your school system requires you call into a phone bank, keep this number and any PINs you may need, along with the substitute contact list.

Documentation is paramount in education. As discussed earlier, when an incident occurs in your classroom, write down the time, date, and nature of the incident immediately. Student behavior and performance should be documented daily. A daily student performance form will help you in achieving this goal.

Each daily student performance form should receive one to three sentence entries per category. Each student should have their own performance sheet with five entries, one for each day of the week. When gathering your weekly materials, make this form part of your routine and keep it in a folder labeled "Student Progress."

Also create a file for each student. Each file will contain parental contacts, incidents, etc. Figure 3.1 is an example of a daily student performance form that you can use to document students' progress.

A template of this sheet is given at the end of this chapter.

The first contact you will have with your students' parents will generally be the first day of school, the week before school starts, or Back-to-School Night. A great way to make a good first impression prior to these

Student Name: Lydia Masao   Week of: October 13, 2008

Date: 10/13/2008
Positive Performance: She answered all of the vocabulary questions correctly, even the words she was previously struggling with.
Behavior: Great day! She showed kindness toward her classmates by complimenting Roger on his drawing.
Area of Improvement: She is struggling with regrouping when subtracting triple-digit numbers.
Notes:

Date: 10/14/2008
Positive Performance: She correctly identified all of the state capitals.
Behavior: Overall good. The PE teacher said she was talking a lot during class.
Area of Improvement: The written paragraph she submitted was sloppily done. Asked her to resubmit.
Notes:

Date: 10/15/2008
Positive Performance: She won the word problem relay.
Behavior: She was not able to participate in the "cook off" during math b/c she would not follow instructions after verbal warning and losing points.
Area of Improvement: Following instructions.
Notes:

Date: 10/16/2008
Positive Performance: She resubmitted a very well written paragraph.
Behavior: Another great day.
Area of Improvement: She is still struggling w/regrouping. A sheet was sent home w/a note to her parents to help her complete and drill.
Notes:

Date: 10/17/2008
Positive Performance: She earned a 90 on her regrouping quiz.
Behavior: She was very kind to her classmates, especially Sam, by offering Sam her eraser to use.
Area of Improvement: The art teacher said she was a chatterbox today in class.
Notes:

FIGURE 3.1
Example of Daily Student Performance Form

would greatly appreciate your completing, a seating chart, and fire drill and evacuation procedures. Please leave me a list of students who followed instructions. I have already let them know that everyone's name should be on the list.

If you have any behavioral problems, please let (teacher's name) know. If the problems persist, please send the student(s) to his/her class. I can be contacted at (your phone number or e-mail address) if you have any questions or concerns.

Once again, I would like to thank you for being my substitute today. Have a great day with the students.

Thanks,

[your name]

STUDENT PERFORMANCE TEMPLATE INTRODUCTORY LETTER

Dear (Parents' and Student's Name),

I am so excited to have you in my class this year! We are going to have so much fun learning about simple machines, dinosaurs, multiplication, ancient Egypt, and so much more. We will also write amazing stories that will be scary, funny, and mysterious throughout the school year. The first day of school is Tuesday, September 6. Back-to-School Night will be Thursday, September 22. We are going to start the school year with the mystery of the missing number. I have enclosed the story of the missing number and a clue.

We will be going on lots of fun field trips this year. The first field trip will be to the Natural History Museum on October 15 for a dinosaur scavenger hunt. I hope you enjoy the rest of your summer.

See you soon,

[your name]

Student Name: _____ Week of: _____

Date: _____
Positive Performance: _____
Behavior: _____
Area of Improvement: _____
Notes:

Date: _____
Positive Performance: _____
Behavior: _____
Area of Improvement: _____
Notes:

Date: _____
Positive Performance: _____
Behavior: _____
Area of Improvement: _____
Notes:

Date: _____
Positive Performance: _____
Behavior: _____
Area of Improvement: _____
Notes:

Date: _____
Positive Performance: _____
Behavior: _____
Area of Improvement: _____
Notes:

Daily Student Performance Form

4

Lesson Plans and Units

Lesson plans and units are to a teacher what a scalpel is to a surgeon. The actual act of teaching is fun and exhilarating, but it cannot happen without a lesson plan or unit. Units are composed of topic-specified lesson plans. In order to create and use successful, effective lesson plans and units, you must:

- know the components of a lesson plan
- create differentiated activities
- use Bloom's Taxonomy
- thoroughly research the topics you are teaching
- incorporate as much technology as possible
- know how to create a cross-curricular unit
- utilize rubrics
- be able to make any adjustments to lessons that the students are having difficulty learning

If you majored in elementary education, you are already familiar with the formal lesson plan. The formal lesson plan contains:

- goals
- objectives

- procedures
- methodology
- evaluation (assessment)
- materials

Some of the components in a formal lesson plan will be part of your informal lesson plans.

Depending on your school system, you may have to submit a formal lesson plan only when you undergo a scheduled observation. If this is the case, ensure that the heading of your lesson plan includes:

- your name
- grade level
- subject
- date
- duration of the lesson

The goal of a lesson is what you want your students to accomplish by the conclusion of the lesson. For example, you may teach students a math lesson in which the goal is that the students have a clear understanding of how to solve multiplication word problems. Goals frequently use abstract words such as *understand, relate,* and *comprehend.* These terms are not easily measured. The goal gives the reader of the lesson plan the whole purpose of the lesson. Think of the goal as the big picture. Goals should be listed first on the lesson plan.

Whereas the goal expresses the big picture, the objectives state specifically to how to achieve the goal. The objectives are the steps the students must take to show that the goal has been achieved. The language for objectives is more concrete and measurable. When writing an objective, always begin with the phrase "Students will be able to. . . ."

The words describing what the student will be able to do to reach the goal are quantifiable. Some of the terms used in expressing objectives are:

- identify
- add
- subtract
- write
- solve
- listen
- read

For example, an objective may be "Students will be able to solve multiplication word problems." You can create an activity that will easily gauge whether students can solve multiplication word problems.

One of the outstanding differences between goals and objectives is that you can easily assess whether your objectives have been achieved in a variety of ways. Most lessons should have two or more objectives; these objectives should be listed after the goal(s) and build upon one another to lead to the achievement of the goal.

The next part of the lesson plan is the procedures. The procedures are the "meat and potatoes" of your lesson as well as the largest portion of the lesson. Procedures are divided into three parts:

- introduction
- instruction
- closure

The introduction of the lesson is important in presenting what the students will be learning and in gauging what they already know about the subject. During the introduction portion, you should ask open-ended questions that require the students to think and apply what they already know. These questions help you measure whether your students have any gaps in their learning about a particular subject.

An example of an open-ended question to ask your students is "How do you solve a multiplication word problem?" Write down all of their suggestions. After identifying what the students know about the subject, introduce new material about the subject. For instance, tell your students, "There are three steps to solving a multiplication word problem." Then place a sign on three students, each detailing a step. Ask the group to put the students with the signs in order. This will transition to the instruction portion of the procedures.

The instruction portion of the procedures is where most of your teaching will be done. You should list, step by step, what you and the students will be doing in this section to reach the objectives. The more explicit you are, the better. The students should be given many examples and opportunities to apply what they are learning.

For example, in the multiplication word problem lesson, students should solve several word problems both as a group and individually. The children should feel free to ask any questions about what they are learning. As the teacher, you must monitor all of the students very closely during this portion of the lesson to assess whether they clearly understand what is being taught, and you should ask many questions to keep students engaged.

I like to think of the instruction portion of the lesson as being on a boat in stormy weather. As the teacher, it is my responsibility to make sure that all the students stay on the boat and don't fall overboard. If any students "fall overboard" because they do not understand the concept, I have to backtrack for these students and present the information again or think of another, more effective way to instruct them.

After the instruction portion is the closure section of the procedures. In the closure section, you will wrap up and reiterate what the students have been taught. In this portion of the lesson, you should ask questions that require the students to summarize and apply what they have just learned.

The next part of your lesson plan, following the procedures portion, is methodology. The methodology describes which methods you used to instruct your students. All learning styles should be engaged. This is the segment of the lesson plan that illustrates whether differentiation is happening in your lesson. Methodology types include:

LESSON PLANS AND UNITS

- direct instruction
- cooperative learning
- discovery learning
- class discussion
- presentation

Evaluation generally follows methodology. The evaluation is how you will assess your students to ensure that the objectives have been mastered and the goals have been reached. The objectives are restated as evaluation statements.

An evaluation statement declares what the student will do as a result of the instruction received. For example, in regard to the multiplication word problems lesson, an evaluation statement would be "Students will solve multiplication word problems." (The objective was "Students will be able to solve multiplication word problems.")

Materials will be the last segment of your formal lesson plan. You should state all the materials necessary to execute the lesson. Once again, you should be as specific as possible when listing and describing the materials needed for the lesson.

This format of a formal lesson plan was what I learned to use in graduate school. Your school system may order or word the sections differently, but the components should remain the same. I have provided the formal lesson plan for Multiplication Word Problems on the following pages. I have also included other formal lesson plans at the end of this chapter.

When writing lessons in your lesson plan book, you should write down the objectives and a very brief explanation of the procedures, materials, and assessments. Before the school year begins, discuss with your grade-level chair what your principal prefers in the lessons you write in your plan book. Follow this advice closely.

Name
Grade
Math
Date
40 minutes

MULTIPLICATION WORD PROBLEMS
1. **Goal**
   - Our goal is to know, understand, and apply the process of solving multiplication word problems.

2. **Objectives**
   - Students will be able to identify the three steps of solving a multiplication word problem.
   - Students will be able to write multiplication sentences for each word problem.
   - Students will be able to solve multiplication word problems.

3. **Procedures**
   A. **Introduction**
      - Ask the students, "How do you solve a multiplication word problem?"
      - Tell the students there are three steps to solving a multiplication word problem.
      - Place a sign listing each multiplication step on each of three volunteers and ask the class which of the step should be first, second, and then third.
   B. **Instruction**
      - Point to the word problem on the board.
      - Ask the students, "What is the first thing you need to do to solve the problem?" Read the problem.
      - Ask, "Would anyone like to read the problem aloud?"

- Ask, "What is the next thing you need to do to solve the problem?" Find a strategy.
- With the class, think of a strategy to solve the problem.
- Ask the class, "What is the last step needed for the word problem?" Solve the problem.
- Use the strategy to solve the word problem.
- Ask the students, "How can you use the information in the problem to write a multiplication sentence?"
- Write a multiplication sentence for the problem.

C. Closure
- Ask the students, "What are the steps to solving a word problem?"
- Ask each table/group to get its word problem answer sheet.
- Assign a sentence strip recorder, word problem sheet recorder, reader, and on-task manager for each table.
- Instruct the students that each group will spend 5 minutes at each word problem station.
- Instruct the students to solve each problem using the steps.
- Instruct the students to write a multiplication sentence for each word problem.

4. Methodology
- Direct instruction
- Cooperative learning
- Discovery learning

5. Evaluation
- Students will identify the three steps of solving a multiplication word problem.
- Students will write multiplication sentences for each word problem on sentence strips.
- Students will solve multiplication word problems.

6. **Materials**
    - Each of the three steps written on three different colored pieces of laminated card stock paper
    - Sheet with word problems
    - Multicolored sentence strips
    - Clipboards
    - Five large sheets of paper with word problems written on them. (These are the word problem stations posted around the room. The word problems will be found at the end of this chapter.)

Differentiated activities are imperative to effective teaching and lesson plans. As discussed earlier, the purpose of differentiated activities is to engage all learners, no matter their individual levels. For example, if you teach a lesson on adjectives in which the students have to brainstorm examples of adjectives, your higher-level learners should be given the task of coming up with more adjectives (e.g., 10) than your lower-level learners (e.g., five).

When you create your lesson plans and activities, keep the learning styles of auditory, visual, and tactile/kinesthetic learners in mind. Just lecturing is no longer acceptable, especially in elementary classrooms.

When you begin planning, review the objectives you will teach your students for each subject over the course of a week. Start brainstorming ideas of activities for each lesson. I suggest having the students engage in activities in which they must create something. To ensure that differentiation is happening, gauge whether each lesson employs all learning styles.

For language arts lessons, if permitted, use centers to ensure movement. During my language arts block, students completed activities with their reading groups. They would rotate to different centers for 30 minutes per center. I had activities at each center based on their reading group. I cannot stress enough how important it is to have students participate in as many hands-on activities as possible. You should keep worksheet activities to a minimum.

When I was in graduate school, my professors strongly emphasized Bloom's Taxonomy, a classification of learning objectives created by Benjamin Bloom and others in the 1950s. I didn't think much of it at the time but gained a healthy respect for it when I started teaching. Bloom's Taxonomy will help you organize the types of activities and lessons you plan in accordance with the effects they will have on the learner.

For instance, if you are teaching your students a unit on Africa, as an activity the students can create a salt map that identifies the different regions and land and water masses and then signify which animals and resources are found in specific regions based on what they have learned. This activity ensures that students will apply the knowledge they have been taught about the physical geography of Africa.

Bloom's Taxonomy is divided into six levels. Each level denotes the level of thinking required by students in mastering a particular concept. The first and lowest level is *knowledge*, or basic recall of information. For instance, in the Africa unit, you can teach your students the names of all of the African countries and their capitals as a particular lesson. At the end of the lesson, you can give the students a test of the country names. Then instruct the students to name the corresponding capital for each country. By having the students name the capital of each country, you are requiring them to do basic recall.

When creating lesson plans, objectives at the knowledge level will state that the student will be able to:

- name
- label
- list
- recognize
- define
- state

The next level of Bloom's Taxonomy is *comprehension*. At this level, students are expected to display a higher level of thinking than the knowledge level. An example of comprehension is to teach the students where each country in Africa is located on a map and to instruct the students about each country's regional area. Afterward, ask the students to identify and locate a country and its corresponding regional area on a blank map. Then ask the students to describe three specific traits about each regional area in Africa.

When creating lesson plans, objectives at the comprehension level will state that the student will be able to:

- identify
- locate
- describe
- explain
- select

Application is the next level in Bloom's Taxonomy. Application requires that the student digest the information given to him or her and then apply it to specific tasks. For example, after you have taught your students about the characteristics of each regional area and country, you can have them play the game "Name That Place."

The students will play as teams that have already been selected based on their table/group assignments. Tell the students that you will give each table the description of a place. If they know the answer, they can name that place. If they don't know the place, they can pass. The other teams will have the opportunity to "buzz in" with the correct answer.

At the end of the game, instruct each student to select his or her favorite place and write a paragraph about it. When creating lesson plans, objectives at the application level will state that the student will be able to:

- solve
- write
- choose
- use
- demonstrate

Analysis follows application in Bloom's Taxonomy. Analysis is usually the highest level most teachers incorporate in their lesson, activities, and assessments. Analysis requires the learner to examine the information and make conclusions. For example, in the Africa unit, the students can do an in-depth study of the governments of two countries in different regional areas.

Afterward, have the students compare and contrast the two governments by highlighting their similarities and differences. At this point, you might use a Venn Diagram to help the students organize their thoughts and translate them into a five-paragraph essay. When creating lesson plans, objectives at the application level will state that the student will be able to:

- compare
- contrast
- differentiate
- examine
- distinguish

Synthesis follows analysis in Bloom's Taxonomy. Synthesis requires the learner to take all the information taught and create something new based on what was learned. For example, at this point in the Africa unit, the students will work within their groups to create a fictional African country. Each group will be given a dossier on its assigned country that includes its location, neighbors, cultural aspects, and resources. Based on this information, each group must decide what type of government its country will have, the services it will provide its people, and its imports and exports. When creating lesson plans, objectives at the synthesis level will state that the student will be able to:

- design
- plan
- create
- develop
- organize

The last and highest level of thinking in Bloom's Taxonomy is *evaluation*. Evaluation requires the learner to take all the information taught and make predictions or arguments. For instance, in the Africa unit, once the students have created and presented their fictional countries, you might give each country a problem that the students must resolve. Instruct the students that they must also predict what will happen to their countries based on the resolution they came up with.

When creating lesson plans, objectives at the evaluation level will state that the student will be able to:

- predict
- assess
- defend
- argue
- estimate

As seen with the examples given in the Africa unit, you must thoroughly research the topics you will teach. We know that the saying "Those who cannot do, teach" is not true; that statement should be modified to "Those who always learn, teach," for you will constantly be learning.

There are many resources available to you as an educator. Your school system employs subject matter experts who can be absolute treasure troves of information. These experts will be able to steer you toward other resources, especially multimedia resources. During the school year, you will be pressed for time, which is why it is best to research topics during the summer.

Your community will also be another great source of information. I was fortunate to teach in the metro D.C. area, which granted me access to the Smithsonian, embassies, think tanks, and much more. The parents will also be a source of information.

One of the best resources for information is technology. Do not be afraid to use technology in your classroom. Podcasts, websites, various software, blogs, DVDs, CDs, smartboards, and the like will make you a better teacher. If you are unsure how to use these various tools, contact the technology specialist at your school or school system. The technology specialist will educate you on how to use technology effectively in your lessons. Your school system should also provide teacher development activities that involve the use of an assortment of technology in your classroom.

As a teacher, you will be required to create units. Cross-curricular units can be a lifesaver. Over the course of the school year, you will be required to teach so many objectives that you simply won't have enough time to do them all individually. This is where cross-curricular units come in. The units will allow you the opportunity and time to combine objectives. The Africa unit is an example of this. We had to teach the seven continents as well as a myriad of different language arts and science objectives. As a result, we created a unit on each continent that encompassed the language arts, social studies, and science objectives.

I have found that basing units on science or social studies topics and objectives is easiest to do. Each unit should not exceed two weeks and should have at least five lessons. I have included an overview of an Ancient Egypt unit at the end of this chapter. A wonderful assessment to culminate a cross-curricular unit is a major project.

When you give your students a project to complete, always give them a rubric to follow. Rubrics are measurements used to determine the grade a student will earn based on the requirements set forth in the rubric. Rubrics are divided into such categories as presentation, visual aid, and essay. Each category will be scored from 3 to 1, with 3 the highest and 1 the lowest score a student can receive. Some rubrics have 4 as the highest score. The rubric will detail exactly what a student must do to receive each score.

Rubrics are important in explaining to students what they must do to receive a certain grade. It takes away the guesswork and can prevent telephone calls from parents who think their children should have received a higher score. An example of a rubric is given in figure 4.1 at the end of this chapter.

Last, what to do when a lesson goes wrong should be considered. When I was student teaching, I did a lesson on measurement. Everything that could go wrong did, and I was being observed by one of my professors. I was absolutely devastated, but I had a great cooperating teacher and wonderful professor. They both explained that lessons will go wrong, but what you do to bounce back is what counts.

You will experience some of these lessons during your teaching career. Your students may not learn anything, but that's OK. Just take a step back and make adjustments. Don't give up on the lesson! Consult your grade-level chair or a master teacher in your school. If the lesson is a math or reading lesson, talk to the math specialist or reading specialist. Once you have decided on the adjustments that need to be made, teach the lesson again. For my lesson gone wrong, I consulted the math specialist at my school, who helped me tremendously.

Teaching the lesson again with adjustments will also serve as an example to your students not to give up on something that doesn't go right the first time you do it. I taught my lesson over with the changes the math specialist suggested, and it was very successful!

QUICK TIPS

- Don't be afraid to duplicate a lesson you have observed.
- One of the greatest resources for creative lesson plans is other teachers.
- Incorporate as much movement into each lesson as possible.
- Allow your students to complete activities on the floor.

LESSON PLANS AND UNITS

In this chapter we discussed the components of a formal lesson plan, differentiated activities, Bloom's Taxonomy, cross-curricular units, and rubrics. Good lesson plans and units are inclusive of all learners, no matter their levels or learning styles. Activities and assessments for lesson plans and units should meet each learner at his or her level.

MULTIPLICATION WORD PROBLEMS

Ms. Masao goes shopping for purses. There is a sale and she buys three purses of six different colors (red, blue, yellow, green, white, and black). How many purses in all did Ms. Masao buy?

Multiplication Sentence: ____ × ____ = _____

Jose finds three types of pens (black, blue, and red). He finds two of each type. How many pens does he have in all?

Multiplication Sentence: ____ × ____ = _____

Crystal, Juanita, Kimberly, Jessica, Jasmine, Amanda, and Ms. Davis go shopping. Each of them buys four shirts. How many shirts do they buy in all?

Multiplication Sentence: ____ × ____ = _____

Brielen opens a store and sells shoes for $10 per pair. She sells nine pairs in one day. How much money does she make that day?

Multiplication Sentence: ____ × ____ = _____

Isreal, Berihu, Liam, and Micheal sell five hats each. How many hats do they sell altogether?

Multiplication Sentence: ____ × ____ = _____

Name
Third Grade
Language Arts: Writing
Date
45 minutes

STUDENT INTERVIEWS
1. **Goal**
   - Our goal is to provide the students with an understanding of the interview process and how to relate this information in a short essay.

2. **Objectives**
   - Students will be able to interview one another using an already formed questionnaire.
   - Students will be able to write a short essay using the information gathered during the interview.

3. **Procedures**

   A. **Introduction**
   - Ask the students, "Can anybody tell me what an interview is?"
   - Ask the students, "Why do we interview people?"
   - Ask the students, "Can you give me an example of an interview you have seen on television or heard?"
   - Tell the students the purpose of interviewing is to find out information and that you can learn interesting facts about a person through an interview.
   - Give the students an interesting fact about yourself to the students; mine is that by the time I was five, I spoke three languages: English, Swahili, and French.

   B. **Instruction**
   - Ask the students, "In order to find out information about someone, we have to ask *what*?"

LESSON PLANS AND UNITS

- Tell the students that in order to have a good interview, you have to have good questions.
- Show the students a questionnaire used to interview another adult (parent volunteer).
- Interview the adult in front of the children.
- Using a projector, model to the students how to write an essay with this information from the interview.

C. Closure
- Cut the following interview-related spelling words in half:
    - interview
    - questions
    - information
    - knowledge
    - report
    - newspaper
    - magazine
    - details
    - article
    - description
- Have each student find the student with the other part of his or her spelling word.
- Explain to each student that he or she will interview and write an essay about whomever matches his or her word
- Give each pair of "matching" students two questionnaires and two sheets to write the essay on.

4. Methodology
    - Class discussion
    - Individual writing
    - Oral interview
    - Modeling

5. **Evaluation**
    - Students will complete the questionnaires.
    - Students will write essays using their questionnaires.
        - Lower-level writers will write one paragraph.
        - Mid-level writers will write two paragraphs.
        - High-level writers will write three paragraphs.
6. **Materials**
    - Questionnaires
    - Writing paper
    - Projector

Name
Fifth Grade
Language Arts: Listening Center
Date
45 minutes

IDIOM HUNT

1. **Goal**
    - Our goal is to provide the students with an understanding of what idioms are and how to use them in their writings.
2. **Objectives**
    - Students will be able to listen to *The Case of the Missing Idioms* at the Listening Center.
    - Students will be able to identify idioms in the story.
3. **Procedures**
    - A. **Introduction**
        - Ask the students, "Who can remind me what an idiom is?"
        - Ask the students, "Who can give me an example of an idiom?"
        - Tell the students that after learning about idioms, they will go on an idiom hunt.

B. **Instruction**
  - Give each table/group two idioms written on 3" × 5" cards, with the meanings written on the backs of the cards.
  - Ask the reader at each table/group to read each idiom aloud.
  - Ask the class what each idiom means.
  - Give the students examples of sentences without idioms.
  - Give the students examples of the same sentences with idioms.
  - Explain to the students that idioms make sentences and stories more interesting.
  - Give each table/group four sentences without idioms written on sentence strips.
  - Give each table/group four idioms written on 3" × 5" index cards.
  - Instruct each table/group to rewrite the sentences using the idioms onto sentence strips.

C. **Closure**
  - Instruct each reading group to listen to *The Case of the Missing Idioms* at the Listening Center.
  - Instruct each reading group to complete the activities/instructions in the group's folder.
    - Lower-level readers will have typed copies of the story and will follow along. At the end of the story, these readers will circle 10 idioms on their typed copies.
    - Mid-level readers will listen to the story and circle at least 15 idioms on copies of the story written on large tablet paper.
    - High-level readers will listen to the story and circle all of the idioms on copies of the story written on large chart paper.

4. **Methodology**
   - Class discussion
   - Discovery learning
   - Cooperative learning

5. **Evaluation**
    - Students will listen to *The Case of the Missing Idioms* at the Listening Center.
    - Students will identify idioms in the story.

6. **Materials**
    - Recording of *The Case of the Missing Idioms*—you will record the story on a blank cassette or CD.
    - Sentence strips
    - Typed copies of *The Case of the Missing Idioms*
    - 3" × 5" index cards with idioms written on the front and their meanings on the back
    - Two copies of *The Case of the Missing Idioms* written on large chart paper

The Case of the Missing Idioms follows.

THE CASE OF THE MISSING IDIOMS

It was a dark and rainy night. It rained so hard that it began raining cats and dogs. I was alone in my office investigating the case of the missing idioms. My name is Ingrid Idiom, and I find idioms. This was a tough case. I had found only one idiom and needed to find three more. Earlier in the week, four idioms had escaped The Big House, a place for naughty idioms that went down the wrong path. They left a note behind that said:

Houston,

We have a problem. We believe that the grass is greener on the other side. There are better things on the horizon for us than this place. We need to return to our lives of glory and live high on the hog again.

Sincerely,

The Escapees

The warden, Mr. Behind Bars, hired me to find the missing idioms. The case was beginning to be harder than a brick wall. I was deep in thought, when suddenly someone began beating my door down.

It was Caught Red-handed, a former resident of The Big House. He had a bad habit of stealing parts of speech. The last I heard, Caught Red-handed was supposed to be in the funny farm. He cracked up after being caught with his hand in the cookie jar stealing nouns that didn't belong to him.

I asked Caught Red-handed, "What can I do for you?" He answered in his raspy voice, "I think I can help you locate the missing idioms." "Oh, really," I suspiciously replied. "What's in it for you?" I asked. "I just want to clear my name," he said. It seemed that Caught Red-handed wanted to turn over a new leaf. I agreed to his much-needed help. I had to face the music. I wasn't getting any closer to finding the other three sneaky idioms.

We soon headed to Wrong Side of the Tracks, the dodgy side of town. Every criminal and lowlife hung out in Wrong Side of the Tracks. We went to It Wasn't Me Pool Hall first to see what we could find.

As soon as we walked in, I noticed two fishy-looking characters laughing and playing the pinball game, The Great Escape. After a closer look, I realized it was none other than those slippery idioms Bad News Travels Fast and Not Playing with a Full Deck. I yelled, "Freeze, Bad News Travels Fast and Not Playing with a Full Deck." They looked stunned and tried to run away, but we were too fast for them.

Later on, Caught Red-handed and I returned them safely to The Big House. I turned to Caught Red-handed and said, "Two down, one to go."

We had no idea where to look next. We soon decided to grab a quick bite to eat at Nina Nouns, the best restaurant in town. Caught Red-handed was on pins and needles around all those nouns, but he got over it.

As we were ordering our dinner, we began to hear the sound of loony laughter coming from the corner table. I went over to get a closer look, when suddenly the culprit flew passed me with his batty giggles. Caught

Red-handed stuck his foot out and tripped him. It was none other than the crazy idiom Mad as a Hatter.

I handcuffed him and said, "It's time for you to go back to the ranch!" He began to laugh uncontrollably and said, "I guess I can't pull the wool over your eyes."

It was a long night, but with the help of a reformed thief, I was able to solve the case of the missing idioms.

Name
Fifth Grade
Language Arts: Writing Center
Date
45 minutes

IDIOM STORY
1. **Goal**
    - Our goal is to provide the students with an understanding what of idioms are and how to use them in their writings.

2. **Objectives**
    - Students will be able to select idioms out of the idiom jar.
    - Students will be able to use the idioms to write a short story at the Writing Center.

3. **Procedures**

    A. **Introduction**
     - Ask the students, "What is an idiom?"
     - Ask the students, "What are examples of idioms?"
     - Tell the students that they will write a short story using idioms.

    B. **Instruction**
     - Go to the idiom jar and select five idioms.
     - Ask for volunteers to read each idiom aloud.
     - Ask the students for the meaning of each idiom.
     - Model the writing process using the idioms in the story.

LESSON PLANS AND UNITS

C. Closure
- Instruct each reading group to follow the instructions in their group folder.
  - Lower-level writers will select three idioms out of the idiom jar and write a short story.
  - Mid-level writers will select five idioms out of the idiom jar and write a short story.
  - High-level readers will select seven idioms out of the idiom jar and write a short story.

4. Methodology
   - Class discussion
   - Discovery learning

5. Evaluation
   - Students will select idioms out of the idiom jar.
   - Students will use the idioms to write a short story at the Writing Center.

6. Materials
   - Chart paper
   - Idioms written on 3" × 5" index cards
   - Small jar

Name
First Grade
Math
Date
45 minutes

MEASUREMENT

1. Goal
   - Our goal is to provide students with an understanding of different ways of measuring volume.

2. **Objectives**
   - Students will be able to identify four units of measurement of volume.
   - Students will be able to differentiate between each of the four forms of measurement.
   - Students will be able to create their own Gallon Guy. The Gallon Guy is a large G filled with four large Qs that represent quarts. Each Q has two Ps that represent pints. Each P contains two Cs that represent cups.

3. **Procedures**

   A. **Introduction**
      - Ask the students, "What does volume mean?"
      - Ask the students, "When would you measure volume?"
      - Ask the students, "Have you ever heard of a cup, quart, pint, or gallon?"
      - Provide each word written on a 3" × 5" index card that can be attached to its corresponding measuring tool.

   B. **Instruction**
      - Tell the students these are units that measure volume.
      - Ask the students, "Would you use these measurements to measure the volume of liquids?"
      - Show the students an 8-ounce cup, a quart, a pint, and a gallon.
      - Attach each card to the correct measurement.
      - Ask the students, "Which of the four is largest?"
      - Divide the students into groups of four, with each student in a group assigned one of the following roles:
        - A: Recorder
        - B: Measurer
        - C: Water Pourer
        - D: Materials Manager/Spokesperson

LESSON PLANS AND UNITS

- Give each group an 8-ounce cup and empty containers that measure 1 pint, 1 quart, and 1 gallon.
- Fill the 1-gallon container halfway with colored water.
- Have each group predict how many cups of water are necessary to fill the pint, quart, and gallon containers.
- The recorders will record the estimates on the charts given to them.
- Each group will then measure out the necessary cups of water needed to fill each container.
- The recorders will record the actual number of cups needed to fill each container.

C. Closure
- After each group finishes recordings, discuss findings as a class.
- Discuss the Gallon Guy with the class.
- Ask the students, "How many cups should go into each pint in the Gallon Guy?"
- Ask the students, "How many pints should go into each quart in the Gallon Guy?"
- Ask the students, "How many quarts should go into the Gallon Guy?"
- Instruct the students to complete measurement questions 1–9 found on page 145 of their math textbooks.
- Instruct each student to create his or her own Gallon Guy.

4. Methodology
   - Discovery learning
   - Cooperative learning

5. Evaluation
   - Students will identify four units of measurement of volume.
   - Students will differentiate between each of the four forms of measurement.
   - Students will create a Gallon Guy.

6. Materials
   - 8-ounce cups
   - pint, quart, and gallon containers for each group
   - charts for each group
   - Gallon Guy

Name
Fourth Grade
Math
Date
60 minutes

ROMAN NUMERALS

1. **Goals**
   - Our goal is to read and understand the value of Roman numerals.

2. **Objectives**
   - Students will be able to understand the value of individual and group Roman numerals.
   - Students will be able to add and subtract Roman numeral values.

3. **Procedures**

   A. **Introduction**
      - Ask the students, "What is a Roman numeral?"
      - Ask the students, "Can you give examples of Roman numerals?"

   B. **Instruction**
      - Using flash cards, introduce each Roman numeral and its assigned value in our numeric system.
      - Explain to the students that a set of Roman numerals is assigned a value that can be calculated by adding the individual numerals together.
      - Instruct the students about the following rules for Roman numerals:
        ○ One numeral cannot be added more than three times. For example, XXX = 30, but XXXX cannot represent 40.

- When a smaller numeral is placed before a larger numeral, you must subtract the smaller number from the larger number. For example, IX = 10 − 1 = 9.
- Ask the students to give the value to a series of Roman numerals.
- Divide the students into six groups of three students each.
- Have each person in the group count from 1 to 3.
- Assign the following roles:
  - 1: materials manager
  - 2: writer (writes down all answers and computations)
  - 3: spokesperson (presents to the class how the group figured out one problem)
- Have the materials manager for each group collect a packet for his or her group containing flash cards that depict the value of each Roman numeral, counters with assigned values written in Roman numerals, and a team worksheet.
- Instruct each group to complete the worksheet provided.

C. Closure
- Have each spokesperson describe how his or her group answered a problem.
- Go over the values once again.
- Play the Roman numeral game.

4. Methodology
   - Presentation
   - Cooperative learning

5. Evaluation
   - Students will understand the value of individual and group Roman numerals.
   - Students will add and subtract Roman numeral values.

6. Materials
   - flash cards
   - worksheets
   - counters with assigned values

Name
Fourth Grade
Math
Date
60 minutes

THE PRICE IS RIGHT
1. **Goal**
   - Our goal is to understand the concept of estimation and its uses.

2. **Objectives**
   - Students will be able to define the term *estimate*.
   - Students will be able to estimate the prices of various items.

3. **Procedures**

   A. **Introduction**
   - Ask the students, "What does the word *estimate* mean?"
   - Ask the students, "When do you have to use estimates?"
   - Ask the students, "Why do you have to be able to estimate?"
   - Give the students real-life examples of when estimation is necessary (e.g., the grocery store).

   B. **Instruction**
   - Divide the students into six groups of three.
   - Ask the students, "Have you ever watched the game show 'The Price Is Right'?"
   - Tell the students that "The Price Is Right" is basically a game show based on estimation.
   - Explain to the students that the team that estimates prices closest to the actual prices will win the game.
   - Have each team estimate the price of an item.
   - The team that comes closest to the actual retail price will play the first game and continue until all teams have the opportunity to play.

- The first game is "High/Low." The students will decide in their groups whether an item's price is higher or lower than the written price. Give the students three items to play this game.
- The second game is "Which Is It?" Give the students the option of two prices for three different items; they must choose the correct price in order to win.
- The third game is "Unscramble the Price." The students must estimate the price of an item by placing the numbers on the board in the correct order.
- The fourth game is "Pick 3." The students must pick three objects out of six within a particular price range. If the students exceed the price of the objects, they lose.
- The fifth game is "Guess the Price." The students must estimate the cost of an item.
- The sixth game is "Pick the Right Number." The students will be given a figure for an item and, for each place value, they must say whether the actual number is one higher or one lower.

C. **Closure**
- End the game by asking the students if they now understand the uses of estimation.
- Ask the students to define the word *estimate*.
- Instruct the students to go back to their seats.
- Instruct the students that they have 15 minutes to estimate the prices of various marked objects.
- Afterwards, discuss the estimations that the students came up with.

4. **Methodology**
   - Discovery learning
   - Cooperative learning

5. **Evaluation**
   - Students will define the term *estimate*.
   - Students will estimate the prices of various objects.

6. **Materials**
   - Timer
   - Items for bidding
   - Note cards
   - Markers

Name
Second Grade
Science
Date
60 minutes

THE SOLAR SYSTEM

1. **Goal**
   - Our goal is to have a basic understanding of our solar system, including the inner and outer planets, the sun, and the asteroid belt.

2. **Objectives**
   - Students will be able to define the term *solar system*.
   - Students will be able to identify the eight planets in our solar system.
   - Students will be able to demonstrate the order in which the planets rotate around the sun.
   - Students will be able to demonstrate the position of the asteroid belt.

3. **Procedures**

   A. **Introduction**
      - Ask the students the following key questions:
        - What is a solar system?
        - How many planets are in our solar system?
        - What are the planets in our solar system?
        - What is the asteroid belt?

- Tell the students that the solar system is a group of heavenly bodies that includes a star, planets, and other objects that orbit that star.
- Use the map of our solar system located in the front of the class for visual reinforcement.
- Tell the class that our star is the sun, and identify the eight planets that orbit the sun.
- Also point out to the students the asteroid belt that separates the inner and the outer planets on the map.

B. Instruction
- Divide the students into five groups of four students each.
- Give each student in each group one of the following roles:
    - Materials manager
    - Cutter
    - On-task manager/planet artist
    - Glitter decorator/gluer
- Have the materials manager collect all the necessary materials for his or her group.
- Have the planet artist in each group draw each planet on STYROFOAM™.
- Have the cutter cut each planet and the sun.
- Have group members discuss among themselves the correct order of the planets; then they will arrange the planets (in order) on their large piece of cardboard (they will also place the sun on the cardboard).
- Have the students mark the area in which the asteroid belt will go.
- After the planets have been correctly arranged, have the gluer glue the sun and the planets to the cardboard.
- The groups will discuss and identify the position of the asteroid belt in their solar system; the glitter decorator will decorate the area of the asteroid belt with gold glitter and glue.

- Have everyone in each group paint the planets with luminescent paint.

C. **Closure**
- While the paint dries, have the students write in their science journals about making the solar system; also have the students define the term *solar system* and identify the eight planets and their order in their journals.
- After the students finish writing in their journals, turn off the lights so that they may be able to see their solar systems glow in the dark!

4. **Methodology**
   - Presentation
   - Cooperative learning

5. **Evaluation**
   - Students will define the term *solar system* in their journals.
   - Students will identify the eight planets in our solar system in their journals.
   - Students will demonstrate the order in which the planets rotate around the sun in their journals and replica of the solar system.
   - Students will be able to demonstrate the position of the asteroid belt on their replica of the solar system.

6. **Materials**
   - Pliable STYROFOAM™
   - Glue
   - Luminescent paint
   - Glitter
   - Cardboard
   - Map of the solar system

Name
Third Grade
Social Studies
Date
45 Minutes

COUNTING IN CHINESE
1. Goal
   - The goal of this lesson is to gain a basic understanding of how to count from one to 10 in Chinese.

2. Objectives
   - Students will be able to verbally count from one to 10 in Chinese.
   - Students will be able to write the numbers one to 10 in Chinese characters.

3. Procedures
   A. Introduction
      - Ask the students, "Have you ever heard of the dialects Mandarin and Cantonese?"
      - Tell the students that these two dialects make up the Chinese language.
   B. Instruction
      - Ask the students to count from one to 10 in English.
      - Have the students repeat each number in Chinese.
      - Show the students the symbol for each letter in Chinese.
      - Divide the students into 4 groups of 5:
         - 1: Materials manager/cover art manager
         - 2: Illustrator
         - 3: Painter
         - 4: Illustrator
         - 5: Painter

- Give each group a counting chart as a guide.
- Each group will make a Chinese counting book that has the English and Chinese translation and the Chinese symbol.

C. **Closure**
  - Use flash cards to quiz the children on counting from one to 10 in Chinese.

4. **Methodology**
   - Presentation
   - Cooperative learning

5. **Evaluation**
   - Students will count aloud from one to 10 in Chinese.
   - Students will write the numbers one to 10 in Chinese characters.

6. **Materials**
   - Flash cards
   - Paint
   - Paintbrushes
   - Bowls
   - Paper
   - Yarn
   - Hole puncher
   - Construction paper
   - Counting chart

ANCIENT EGYPT UNIT OVERVIEW
Grade Level: Third

Days 1–2:   Introduction to Ancient Egypt

Objective: The students will be able to identify and describe major components of the Ancient Egypt civilization:

- mummification
- pharaohs

- gods and goddesses
- pyramids
- hieroglyphics
- the Rosetta Stone
- the discovery of Tutankhamen's tomb

Activities: Divided into groups of three, the students will use an Ancient Egypt Webquest to answer questions related to the aforementioned topics.

Day 3: Pyramids

Objectives:

1. The students will be able to identify uses of pyramids.
2. The students will be able to identify mastabas as the early pyramids.
3. The student will be able to create pyramids.

Activities:

- Using the Webquest as an informational tool, students will answer questions in their teams about pyramids.
- Each team will create pyramids using sugar cubes.

Day 4: Mummies

Objectives:

1. The students will be able to describe the use of mummification in Ancient Egyptian society.
2. The students will be able to briefly describe the process of mummification.

Activities:

- Using the Webquest as an informational tool, students will answer questions in their teams about mummification.
- Each team will create papier-mâché mummies with bodies molded out of white molding.

Days 5–6: Hieroglyphics

Objectives:

1. The students will be able to identify hieroglyphics as the writing system used by the Ancient Egyptians.
2. The students will be able to identify the Rosetta Stone as a key that helped archaeologists decode the meaning of hieroglyphics.

Activities:

- Using the Webquest as an informational tool, students will answer questions in their teams about hieroglyphics.
- Each team will create a painted hieroglyphic book in the style of an alphabet book.

Days 7–9: Famous Pharoahs

Objectives:

1. The students will be able to identify the rulers of Ancient Egypt as pharaohs.
2. The students will be able to research a famous pharaoh using an Ancient Egypt website.

Activities:

- Using the Webquest as an informational tool, students will answer questions in their teams about pharaohs.
- Each team will have a choice of the following pharaohs: Tutankhamen, Ramses II, and Cleopatra, and they will research five facts about their chosen pharaoh.
- Each team will create a HyperStudio stack using the five facts about the group's selected pharaoh.

Days 10–12: Physical Ancient Egypt

Objectives:

1. The students will be able to identify Ancient Egypt as a part of the African continent.
2. The students will be able to identify the cities of Thebes and Memphis as major cities in Ancient Egypt.
3. The students will be able to identify the Nile River as an important source of water.

Activities: Each team will create and decorate a salt map of Africa that correctly identifies the Nile River, Memphis, and Thebes.

Evaluations/Assessment:

- Students will be assessed by how well they participate in their groups.
- The groups will be assessed by the various rubrics.
- The HyperStudio projects will be graded by their accuracy.

Areas	1	2	3
Map	There is no decoration.	The whole map is painted. Slightly neat and little decoration.	Various colors are used to indicate water and land masses. Very neat. Attention to detail and decorative.
Cities	Not shown or shown in incorrect geographical locations.	1 city shown in correct location	Memphis and Thebes shown in correct locations. Distinctive from other landmarks.
The Nile	Not shown.	N/A	The Nile River is shown in its correct location.

FIGURE 4.1
Ancient Egypt Salt Map Rubric

II
ROUTINES, RULES, AND REINFORCEMENT

5

Routines

One of the primary building blocks to good classroom management is routine. Routines should be simple and planned in advance. Good routines require setting schedules, creating and modeling simple procedures, consistency, and using dead time.

Before the school year begins, consult with your grade-level team or principal about general instructional times for various subjects, the order of learning blocks, any requirements for instructional times, and the mandatory amount of recess for your grade level. I taught at a traditionally based school. As a result, our language arts block was in the morning and math was in the afternoon. We taught science and social studies between these two blocks.

Most school systems require two hours for the language arts block and one and one half hours for the math block. As a classroom teacher, you may be required to have your students write and read silently for a prescribed amount of time daily. If you teach in the primary grades, you may be required to read aloud to your students for a set amount of time each day.

Your school system may also require that your students have at least 15 minutes of recess per day. This basic schedule, along with the times

Daily Schedule	
8:20–8:45:	Morning Work
8:45–9:00:	Review Daily Checklist/Morning Warm-Up
9:00–11:00:	Language Arts
11:00–12:00:	Lunch/Recess
12:05–12:50:	Specials
12:55–1:30:	Science
1:30–2:05:	Social Studies
2:05–3:10:	Math
3:10–3:15:	Clean-Up
3:20:	Dismissal

FIGURE 5.1
Example of a Daily Schedule

your class is assigned to go to specials (art, music, physical education, etc.), will set the platform for your daily instructional schedule. Stay within the parameters set by your principal and grade-level chair.

After creating your daily schedule, post it at the front of your classroom. Figure 5.1 provides an example of a daily schedule.

You should adhere to your schedule as much as possible. I suggest giving group restroom breaks after morning work, before and after lunch, and after specials. You should also post a specials schedule next to your daily schedule, so the children will know which specials they go to daily. Figure 5.2 provides an example of a specials schedule.

Simple daily procedures are as important as schedules. Before the school year begins, you should create procedures for:

- morning start-up
- submitting homework
- submitting classwork
- restroom breaks
- going to lunch
- transitioning to and from centers
- reading groups
- lining up in the classroom
- walking in the hallways
- returning from recess
- dismissal

These procedures should never be "played by ear."

Starting with the first day of school, you should discuss with your students the procedures you want them to follow and model them.

Specials Schedule		
Monday:	Art	12:00–12:50
Tuesday:	P. E.	12:00–12:30
Wednesday:	Music	12:00–12:50
Thursday:	P. E.	12:00–12:30
Friday:	Library	12:00–12:50

FIGURE 5.2
Example of a Specials Schedule

Give your students procedures in simple steps. You can write down the steps and/or explain them verbally. Practice and constant reinforcement will ensure that your students will follow all procedures. The first 4–6 weeks of school will be spent setting expectations and teaching classroom procedures.

Morning start-up will be the way your students will begin each day in your classroom. The following is an example of the morning procedures my students had to follow when first entering the class:

1. Put away your backpack and coat in the closet.
2. Get your chair and place it at your desk.
3. Get a pencil from the pencil box.
4. Complete your morning work.
5. Place your completed morning work in your table's tray.

Note that morning work should review previously taught skills. The morning work for my students consisted of math problems, daily oral language, and a fun fact. After your students complete and submit their morning work, instruct them to read until time to review the daily checklist. If a student completes all of his or her work during a learning block and has no prior work to complete from that block, instruct him or her to read silently at his or her desk or in the classroom library.

The simpler the procedures, the more quickly and easily your students will adhere to them. Try to create procedures that do not exceed more than five steps. The only way your students will follow procedures correctly will be to do them over and over again during the first few weeks of school.

If not properly created and enforced, bathroom procedures can become the bane of a teacher's existence. Children will unnecessarily ask to use the bathroom as much as possible if you allow them. By having group restroom breaks, you can reduce the number of individual restroom breaks and model the behavior you want students to exhibit when they go individually.

Explain and model for the students early on the procedures they must follow. If you want to provide your students with a bathroom pass, explain the procedures for using the pass and the amount of times they are limited to its use.

Routines cannot work without consistency: do not waffle. Make your plan and stick to it. There is always room to tweak your procedures, but unless they are completely useless, do not get rid of them all together. Drill, drill, drill will be the order of the day until your students are able to seamlessly follow all classroom procedures.

During the course of the school day, there will be moments that I call *dead time*. Dead time is the time when students are not engaged in an activity, and this can open the door to problems. Dead time usually occurs when the students are standing in line, waiting in the hallway to use the restroom, or waiting for a schoolwide assembly to start. Children who are easily distracted have the most problems with dead time.

When students are bored, they tend to misbehave, and dead time will lead to misbehavior. During these times, you should engage your students in math drills or question-and-answer sessions. Ask the students questions about various topics currently being taught in the class. For instance, if your students are learning about the state capitals, ask each student to give you the capital of a different state or the state of a different capital. Using dead time for instructional time makes every moment a teachable moment.

In this chapter we discussed the importance of routine in an organized classroom. Good routines consist of simple procedures and constant reinforcement. There should be procedures in place for submitting work, lining up, using the restroom, and more. An effective teacher clearly explains and models the procedures he or she expects students to follow.

QUICK TIPS

- Don't be afraid to have your students practice often how they should line up and walk in a line the first weeks of the school year.
- Remember that when your students and you are in the hallways for restroom breaks, to go to lunch, or to go to specials, your principal will be watching to see how well-behaved your students are.
- Nothing annoys a principal more than to see and hear rowdy students in the hall.
- When the class is working on a whole group activity, ask the students who are finished to put their right thumbs in the air to let you know they are done.
- Be specific—never assume that your students will know what to do, especially in the primary grades.

6

Rules

Rules are the cornerstone of every classroom. They establish order and set expectations. Rules should be few in number, positively stated, accompanied with consequences, and clearly explained with examples of situations.

Many teachers, especially first-year teachers, make the common mistake of creating too many classroom rules. The rule of thumb should be no fewer than three rules and no more than five. This allows students to learn and apply the rules quickly and effectively.

After pinpointing the number of rules you will have in your classroom, decide which positive behaviors you would like to see exhibited most. Write these behaviors down and use them as a template in writing the classroom rules. These rules should always be positively stated in sentences that begin with the word "I." This gives students ownership and responsibility for their behavior.

Below is an example of positively stated classroom rules:

1. I will raise my hand to share.
2. I will respect my classmates and myself.
3. I will follow all directions.
4. I will listen while others are talking.

Do not create classroom rules that are negatively stated. The rules should always focus on what the students will be expected and required to do in your classroom. When rules are stated positively, students are given a template of the behavior they will exhibit in your classroom.

In order for rules to be effective, there must be consequences. It is not advisable to have more consequences than rules, because it will foster a punitive environment. Consequences should also be clearly stated and correlate to your behavior management system. When presenting consequences to your students, let them know they will always have the opportunity to "make it right." The following are examples of consequences:

- verbal warning
- written warning
- phone call home
- trip to the principal's office

Making it right is all about getting a second chance. It allows students to redeem themselves. Remember the student in your classes in elementary school who always got into trouble? This was the child who seemed to make your teacher's day a living nightmare. He or she quickly got the label of the "bad kid" and always had a look of resignation that all he or she would ever be in school was the bad kid. As a result, this child was probably mildly ostracized by the other children.

When we hear stories about students being ostracized by their teachers and peers, we always say, "I would never do that." The truth is that you probably will if you don't put a system in place that allows students to correct bad choices. There will be days when children's behavior will drive you to some mild form of madness, but remember to give them the opportunity for a redo.

By giving your students the opportunity to correct their mistakes, you let them know that they are not bad, but the choice they made was bad. Distinguishing that for your students is very important. Engage your students by asking them what they can do to make things right when they break a particular rule.

The first consequence to breaking a rule should be a verbal warning. When giving the warning, engage the student in the process by asking which rule he or she may be breaking. As he or she responds, let the student know that you are issuing a verbal warning and ask what he or she can do to rectify the situation.

For example, if a student blurts out an answer without permission, ask the student, "Should you be calling out the answer?" After he or she responds, ask the student which rule is being broken and why. Then tell the student, "I am giving you a verbal warning, but what can you do from now on if you want to say the answer?" The student's response should hit upon following the rule that was broken.

At that moment, take the opportunity to praise the child for knowing this and let him or her know that you expect him or her to follow the rule. An example of an appropriate response is "Good thinking! I am glad you know to raise your hand to share. And I know you will do this from now on."

Let the student know that you cannot wait until he or she has the opportunity to follow the rule. By having this response, you will be positively reinforcing the rule and the thought process that your students must engage in to follow the rules. As soon as the student follows the rule, acknowledge what he or she has done by praising him or her.

The next consequence should be a written warning. The written warning recommended is not the typical written warning used by most educators. It is a laminated strip of brightly colored paper with the word "WARNING" written in bold, uppercase letters on it. You should create at most 10 warning strips.

Explain to your students that if an inappropriate behavior, such as yelling out the answer, continues, they will be given a written warning to place on their desks. At this point, ask your students how they can correct the inappropriate behavior. Let them know that when they take action to correct the behavior, you will not only take back the warning but also reward them according to the behavior management system. This will be an opportunity for them to redeem themselves.

The next consequence should correlate to your behavior management system. If your students are earning points or popsicle sticks (discussed further in Chapter 8, "Creating Behavior Management Systems"), take away 1–2 points or bucks. When you take a student's points or bucks away, let him or her know the rule he or she is breaking and ask how he or she can earn the points or bucks back. This is the same principle used when giving the verbal warning. Always give your students the opportunity to redeem themselves.

The final consequence should be parental contact or a trip to the principal's office, in that order. This should always be a *last* resort. Your students will have "off" days, but give them the opportunity to get back on track by going to the Quiet Corner or using the Letting Out My Feelings Book or Daily Classroom Journal. When all these avenues have been exhausted, let the student know that you will be contacting his or her parent.

When contacting a parent, give the parent a brief synopsis of what has happened and what steps were taken. Briefly discuss what can be done by the student to prevent the behavior from happening. By giving the parents a plan of action, you are less likely to sound accusatory and they are more likely to respond positively and productively in preventing the behavior from reoccurring.

You should have the student present when you make the phone call to parents. This will give the parents an opportunity to speak to the student. Try to end the call on a positive note of moving forward.

A trip to the principal's office is never a good thing. I rarely took children to see the principal and only in extreme situations. By avoiding such trips, I showed my principal that I was in control of my classroom. When you do have to go, document the incident and the original steps taken before going and share it with the principal upon arrival.

Rules and consequences should be posted side by side in your classroom. I usually made a small laminated copy of the rules and consequences for each student to keep at his or her desk. This is a great

Rules	Consequences
1. I will raise my hand to share.	1. Verbal Warning
2. I will follow all directions the first time they are given.	2. Written Warning
	3. Phone Call Home
3. I will respect my classmates and myself.	4. Trip to the Principal's Office
4. I will listen while others are talking.	** I always have the chance to make it right! **
5. I will use my inside voice when sharing.	

FIGURE 6.1
Example of Classroom Rules and Consequences

reference tool for students when a verbal or written warning is given. Figure 6.1 provides an example of classroom rules and consequences side by side.

An effective tool in presenting and implementing rules and consequences is scenarios. Scenarios allow the students to understand various situations in which rules can be broken. For each rule, give the students a scenario in which the rule is broken. Question and engage the students in a discussion about how the rule was broken and the proper consequence for each situation. Examples of scenarios and their correlating questions are given at the end of this chapter.

Another way to implement rules is through role-playing. Your school's guidance counselor is a great resource for applying role-playing in your classroom. Discuss with him or her different role-playing exercises that can be done in your classroom to teach your students about rules and their importance. Role-playing can also be used to discuss particular situations, such as death, divorce, and abuse.

As discussed earlier, your students will have "off" days. As a teacher, you will have to be able to infer whether something is wrong with the student or whether he or she is just having a bad day. Your students may be having problems in their homes, or they may be hungry, not feeling well, or just tired. You need to be sensitive to any of these scenarios and act accordingly.

The longer you teach, the greater your teacher's intuition will become. Remember to give your students a certain amount of leeway, because your classroom may be the only safe place they have, whether you teach in affluent or poor schools.

During my first year of teaching, I had a student who was usually very sweet and kind to her classmates. One day she came into the classroom and was being very mean to everyone. She even made her best friend cry. This was completely out of character for her. I took her aside and asked what was wrong. After talking for a while, I found out she was hungry. I gave her two graham crackers and she got back on track.

In this chapter we discussed rules, their corresponding consequences, and implementing them. Rules should always be positively stated and begin with the word "I." You should not have fewer than three or more than five rules in your class. You should also try to have fewer consequences than rules. Always give your students the opportunity to make it right.

SCENARIO ONE

Rebecca's mother bought her new pencils that were made of different colors. Rebecca sat next to John, who really liked the pencils. Rebecca had seven pencils, and John asked if he could have a pencil, but she said no. This made John very angry. Rebecca had seven pencils, and she couldn't use them all at the same time. John decided to take a pencil while Rebecca wasn't looking. When Rebecca returned to her desk, she

> **QUICK TIPS**
>
> - Be sensitive to your students and their needs.
> - When correcting your students, use a firm but gentle tone of voice. Don't yell. Adults don't respond well to yelling, and children don't, either.
> - If you have a student who is having behavioral difficulty and you suspect troubles at home, talk to your school guidance counselor, principal, grade-level chair, or a master teacher you trust.
> - When students are having an off day and difficulty following the rules, allow them the opportunity to get it back together.

saw that one of her pencils was missing. She told her teacher and started to cry.

Questions:

- Why was Rebecca upset?
- What rule did John break?
- How was taking Rebecca's pencil not being respectful?
- Were Rebecca's feelings hurt?
- How do you know her feelings were hurt?
- When you hurt someone's feelings, is that being disrespectful, too?
- What is the first consequence?
- What would be the next consequence?
- Should John get the chance to make it up to Rebecca?
- How can she make it up to him?

SCENARIO TWO

Ms. Williams' class was building a paper pyramid. It was almost time for lunch. She told her students to clean up their areas and put their paper pyramid materials away in their cubbies. She also told the class that the table with the cleanest area would get a prize. Lisa was almost finished with her paper pyramid. All she had left to do was finish gluing the last side. Lisa thought that since she was almost done, she could just keep working. While Lisa continued to work, everyone at her table cleaned up and put away their paper pyramids.

Questions:

- Do you think Lisa's table won the prize? Why or why not?
- What rule did Lisa break?
- Was it OK for Lisa to keep working, even though she was almost done?
- Would you have done what Lisa did?
- If you were at Lisa's table, would you be mad at her for not winning the prize?
- Even if you are mad at Lisa, is it OK to hurt her feelings?
- Would hurting Lisa's feelings break any rules?
- Which rule would be broken?
- Describe a situation when people in your class got mad at you.

SCENARIO THREE

Every Monday, Mr. Lee let his students share one thing they did over the weekend with the class. Pete couldn't wait to share. Pete and his dad had gone camping in the woods and had seen a real bear. The bear even growled at them and stood straight up! There were so many kids in line to share their stories before him, and he really wanted to tell his story. Everyone in the class had known Pete was going camping, and he promised to tell them if he had any adventures. The more he thought about the big bear showing all of its big, scary teeth, the more he wanted to tell his story. While Karen was telling everyone about her family barbecue, Pete couldn't take it any longer. He yelled out, "I saw a bear in the woods and it was going to attack us!"

Questions:

- What rule did Pete break?
- What could Pete have done instead of yelling out?
- Pete had a very exciting story to tell—does that excuse breaking the rule?

7

Reinforcement

Two types of reinforcement will occur in your classroom: positive and negative. Positive reinforcement reinforces a positive behavior such as following directions. Negative reinforcement reinforces negative behaviors. In order to have a well-managed classroom, you must consistently reinforce positive behaviors and use alternatives to negative reinforcement.

It is easy to get into the trap of noticing only negative behaviors; try to avoid this. Every child can behave positively, and you must constantly and consistently praise those behaviors when they occur. Verbal praise is one of the greatest positive reinforcement tools. Use verbal praise generously in your classroom, especially at the beginning of the school year. Examples of verbal praise are:

- I like the way Caroline is sitting quietly.
- I like the way John is following directions.
- You are being a good listener.
- You are showing great pride in your work.

When giving your students verbal praise, specify a rule and particular behavior that you want to reinforce. The more you praise a behavior, the more your students will repeat it. Another way to verbally praise your students is to call their parents when they exhibit the positive behaviors you are trying to reinforce. When you call the parent, make sure the student is there and has the opportunity to hear you sing his or her praises and talk to his or her parent.

Another form of positive reinforcement is tangible rewards. These are rewards that your students can put their hands on. Tangible rewards that will be given in your class should come from your behavior management system and any extras, such as good notes to take home or an "I'm Having a Great Day" award. It is very important to communicate to parents and students as much as possible when they are having a good day. Examples of tangible rewards are:

- stickers
- good notes home
- lunch bunch (the students eat lunch with you)
- food
- extra recess
- a class party

Children tend to covet good notes home. I had stationery in the shape of an apple in my classroom. Each day I would take two to three sheets from the pad and hang them on the whiteboard. I would inform my students of the number of good notes I would be giving away that day when we went over our daily checklist. The students would work hard toward getting one of these notes.

Throughout the course of the day, I would distribute the blank notes to students who earned them. As I gave them the notes, I would tell them why they were receiving a good note home. At the end of the day, before dismissal, I would write each note, detailing what the student did to earn the note. The children, and their parents, would enjoy reading them.

Intrinsic rewards—rewarding yourself for doing a good job—are also positive reinforcement. You should do a good job not because you want someone to praise you or because you want a big reward but simply because you expect that of yourself. Everything discussed in this book so far allows students the ability to reward themselves intrinsically. By setting high standards, helping them meet these standards, and praising them when they do meet these standards, you put students on the path of giving themselves intrinsic rewards.

As stated earlier, negative reinforcement reinforces negative behavior. When you bring attention to and focus on a negative behavior, you reinforce it. There are alternatives to negative reinforcement that you should use in your classroom. These alternatives include ignoring the behavior, physical proximity, redirecting inappropriate behaviors into positive behaviors, and separation.

The first line of defense in dealing with a negative behavior is to simply ignore it. There are times when students will participate in negative behaviors simply for attention. By choosing to ignore the behavior, you do not reinforce it but, rather, steer the student toward cessation of the behavior.

For example, I had a student who talked incessantly. I finally moved her desk near mine, which is where she wanted to be. Instead of talking to her classmates, she started talking to me. When I ignored the constant chatter, it stopped. The student wasn't getting much attention at home, as her mother had just given birth to twins and she was now the "middle child." I set aside time to spend with her one on one. She had to work toward this one-on-one time by reducing the chatter, and eventually she was able to move back to her table.

Physical proximity requires getting close to a student while the inappropriate behavior is occurring. You are not verbally acknowledging the behavior but, instead, by standing near the student, you are giving the cue that the behavior is unacceptable and must stop.

The "look" is usually used in conjunction with physical proximity. All teachers and parents master the "look," which basically lets the student know to stop. When students are talking during a lesson or doing something other than what they are supposed to be doing, the "look" is the best way to redirect without saying anything about the behavior.

Redirection is one of my favorite alternatives to negative reinforcement. One of my students had difficulty with any sort of change or variance to his schedule. Due to a snowstorm, he was unable to attend a play date that was scheduled for that afternoon. He made it abundantly clear to me and anyone else listening that he was not happy with the situation by constantly complaining. Every time he would issue a complaint, I would counter with a positive statement about him. Each time I did this, he would stop complaining, until the complaining ceased entirely that day. Redirection requires patience and time but will yield positive results.

Separation is used when the other alternatives have been exhausted. When you separate a student from the rest of the group, explain clearly to the student why he or she is being separated. Ask the student what he or she can do to be part of the classroom community again. This allows the student to come up with a plan of action that he or she is responsible for and to redeem him or herself.

In this chapter, we discussed the two types of reinforcement: positive and negative. Positive reinforcement includes verbal praise, tangible rewards, and intrinsic rewards. Alternatives to negative reinforcement are ignoring the behavior, physical proximity, the "look," redirection, and potentially separation.

QUICK TIPS

- Don't forget the quiet students in your class. It will be easy to overlook them at times because they will follow directions and do a great job, but always make an effort to praise their quiet efforts.
- Use kindness when dealing with your students.
- The idea that sticks and stones will break your bones but words will never harm you is a fallacy. Words can stay with a child for a lifetime, so always use positive words.
- If you tell your students you are going to do something, do it. Mean what you say and say what you mean.

III

BEHAVIOR MANAGEMENT SYSTEMS

8

Creating Behavior Management Systems

A behavior management system is the final component in creating an ordered classroom. A good behavior management system will provide your students with a template of the standards of your classroom and how to reach them. These standards will include how they should interact with one another and with you and the work ethic you would like them to demonstrate. When creating a behavior management system, always make certain that it:

- is simple
- sets attainable goals
- sets attainable behavioral objectives
- is precise in defining rules
- is precise in defining consequences
- is precise in defining rewards

When introducing the system to your students, model it thoroughly.

Before the beginning of the school year, create an individual behavior management system for your students. In an individual-based system, students are accountable only for themselves. This approach will acclimate them to the rules, consequences, and behavioral objectives you want them to learn.

Individual systems also help students rise to the classroom standards and expectations you have set. The students must have a clear understanding of the system in order for it to be effective. As a means of reducing your workload, create an individual system that can also easily transition to a group management system.

As the year proceeds, you will be able to identify which students excel in certain areas and struggle in others. This information will help you to organize your students in a group setting that is most conducive to learning. A group-based management system will foster a positive team dynamic and teach your students to work effectively with one another. Examples of both plans are given in Chapter 9, "Individual Plans and Group Plans."

You will encounter students who are completely resistant to both the individual and group management systems you have created. For these students, a universal behavior plan will be necessary. The universal behavior plan is discussed in further detail in Chapter 10, "The Universal Behavior Plan."

Before creating your system, key questions must be answered to ensure its effectiveness. These questions include:

- Which behavioral objectives would you most like the system to reinforce?
- How will your students be rewarded for exhibiting these behaviors?
- Will the students have to accrue something to be rewarded? For instance, will they have to accrue a particular number of points, stickers, classroom cash, or popsicle sticks?
- How many points, stickers, etc. will your students have to accumulate before being rewarded? (This will be their goal.)
- How much time will you give them to reach the goal? (Will the rewards be earned weekly, biweekly, or monthly?)
- In what type of increments will the points, stickers, etc. be distributed to the students?

CREATING BEHAVIOR MANAGEMENT SYSTEMS   117

- Will there be certain behaviors that receive more points, stickers, etc. than others?
- How will you record how many points, stickers, etc. your students have earned?
- What rewards will you give your students for reaching their goal?

Simplicity is essential when creating behavior management systems, especially in the early elementary grades (K–2). As a point of reference, your students should be able to summarize the system in five sentences or fewer. To ensure that your behavior plan remains simple, write down the steps the students must follow to participate positively in the plan. Limit these steps to no more than five and record each step on a sentence strip. The strips will be used when introducing and modeling the system to your students. Afterward, post them next to the classroom rules and consequences.

I also recommend typing a copy of the steps in a small box like the one used for the daily checklist, photocopying one for each student, laminating each copy, and distributing them to the students to keep on their desks. These will serve as a visual reminder to each student.

At the beginning of the year, you should set weekly goals for students to achieve. As the year progresses, you can transition the students to biweekly or monthly goals. The goals will be based on what you have decided your students need to accrue (points, popsicle sticks, classroom cash, stickers, etc.). Begin your weekly goals with an easily attainable number. For instance, you may require your students to earn 50 points the first week of school to get the weekly reward. Each week, the goal should be higher than the previous week's goal. For example, if the weekly goal for students one week is 60 points, the weekly goal for the following week should be at least 70 points.

The weekly goals will be achieved by following the classroom rules and accomplishing the behavioral objectives you have set. The behavioral objectives can be extrapolated from your classroom rules and any other behaviors your want to work on. Behavioral objectives must be specific and positively stated. The following are examples of behavioral objectives:

- I raise my hand to share.
- I stay on task and neatly complete my assignments.
- I use good manners by saying please and thank-you.
- I follow all instructions the first time they are given in class and specials.
- I stand and walk quietly in line.

Whenever a student reaches one of these objectives during the course of the week, immediately give him or her the points, stickers, etc. earned. Let students know how many points they can earn for achieving each objective. Be consistent and diligent in this process. Also, advise your students that it is always best to earn more points, etc. than they need.

Whatever you choose for your students to accrue, decide how you and the students will store and keep track of it. For instance, if your students accumulate popsicle sticks, you can give each child a cup with his or her name written on it to house the popsicle sticks. The cups should be kept on the students' desks so that they have a visual reminder of what they have and what they need to meet the weekly goal.

I recommend that students count how many points, stickers, popsicle sticks, etc. they have accrued midweek. This will reinforce the goal they have to reach and push them toward reaching it. Remind the students of how they can earn additional points, stickers, etc. Review the behavioral objectives with the students.

Your classroom rules and consequences are an integral part of the management system. When presenting the system to your students, begin by discussing the rules of the class. As discussed in Chapter 6, scenarios are an effective way to present and clarify classroom rules and their consequences.

Engage the students in a discussion about how the rules can be followed. During the discussion, ask the students why they think each rule is important and give them examples. Ask the students to restate the rules and consequences in their own words. By doing this, you show that the rules do not have to be followed simply because you say so but, rather, that they have true merit.

Your students must have a clear understanding of the rules and consequences in action in the classroom. One of the greatest ways to ensure that your students clearly understand the rules and the system is to begin using the system from the first moment the students enter your classroom. Explain to the students that you will always be on the lookout to reward those who are following the rules. Examples of classroom rules and consequences are listed in Chapter 6.

The final ingredient in the behavior management system is the rewards. Make a list of the rewards you want your students to earn. Then rank the rewards from highest to lowest. More valuable rewards should have higher weekly goals. Since you will be starting the school year with weekly goals, rewards should be distributed on Fridays. Variety stores, such as Dollar General, are great places to purchase inexpensive rewards. The following are examples of rewards:

- popcorn
- 5 minutes of extra recess
- a pencil
- lunch bunch: you eat lunch with the winners
- popsicles
- a book
- a homework pass

After you have created your behavior management system, briefly write a synopsis of the plan. Give the synopsis to your principal, and explain the finer points of the plan. This will enable your principal to know what system you are using, especially if a parent contacts him or her and asks about the plan you have in place.

The success of your behavior management system is dependent on its simplicity, the ability of your students to navigate it effectively, and your consistent reinforcement. There is no room for generalities in your system; it must be clear and concise. You must also give the system time to take effect. Always be on the lookout for behavior that you can positively reinforce verbally and through your system. Do *not* start your behavior system after the first day of school.

In this chapter, we discussed the key elements in creating a behavior management system: simplicity, setting attainable goals and behavioral objectives, and defining rules and consequences. An individual behavioral system should be put in place and utilized on the first day of school. The system will set the expectations your students must meet. As the year progresses, transition to a group behavior system to promote cooperative learning.

QUICK TIPS

- The first week of school will center on learning and retaining classroom procedures. Your system should be used to positively reinforce the procedures by setting a goal that everyone can reach.
- Always seek out and reward students who are following the classroom rules and achieving the behavioral objectives.
- Be diligent with your system.
- When you get your class list, do not make the mistake of consulting the teachers of your students from the previous year.
- Allow each student to have a clean slate with you when he or she begins the school year in your classroom.

9

Individual Plans and Group Plans

As discussed in Chapter 8, you should begin the school year with an individual behavior plan for your students. Once you get a clear assessment of which students will work best together, transition to a group plan. It is preferable, but not necessary, to create an individual plan that can transition to a group plan. If your individual plan cannot be used as a group plan, create a group plan that defines the classroom rules and consequences as well as sets the behavioral objectives you want your students to reach.

Your behavioral objectives may change during the course of the year. In the following pages, detailed examples of individual and group plans are given. These can serve as a springboard for you, or you can use them in their entirety in your classroom. Additional strategies for students with special needs or disabilities are also provided.

INDIVIDUAL PLANS

The Stamp Card

Procedures

Each student is given a card on Monday mornings. The card will list:

- days of the week
- classroom rules written as behavioral objectives

- an area for parents' signatures
- student's learning blocks
- weekly goal

The weekly goal should also be written on the board.

If a student reaches all of his or her behavioral objectives in a particular time slot, the student receives a stamp for his or her card. If the student does not reach the behavioral objectives in a particular time slot, after two warnings (verbal and written), the numbers of the behavioral objectives not reached are written on the card instead. The card will be kept on top of the student's desk.

At the end of the day on Fridays, the students will count the number of stamps they have earned. Students who have reached the weekly goal will receive the weekly reward. The cards should be collected and placed in the students' mailboxes to be sent home in the weekly take-home folders. Parents should sign and return the cards. The signed cards, which will be useful as documentation, should be filed in the students' files. Figure 9.1 at the end of this chapter provides a template of a stamp card. This system should be used at the beginning of the year.

Materials

The materials needed for this system are:

- brightly colored card stock
- stamps
- ink pads
- weekly rewards

Classroom Cash

Procedures

In the classroom cash system, students will earn classroom money to reach their weekly goals. This system not only works as a behavior management plan but also reinforces mathematical and economic skills, such as:

- counting money
- buying and selling goods
- maintaining a bank account
- counting change

Each student will have his or her own bank account to maintain money earned. The teacher serves as the banker.

In this system, each classroom rule and behavioral objective will have an assigned cash value. You should compile a list of the behavioral objectives along with the classroom rules and order them from most valuable to least valuable.

You may decide to use whole dollar values ($1, $2, $3, etc.), change values (25¢, 50¢, 75¢, etc.), or a combination (which is most advisable for second through fifth grades). You should give each student a typed, laminated list to keep on their desks, and a classroom copy of the list should be placed in a highly visible area. Listed below are examples of rules and objectives and their cash values:

- I follow instructions when they are given: $2
- I am kind and respectful toward my classmates: $2
- I listen while others are talking: $2
- I turn in neat and well-done assignments: $1.50
- I raise my hand to share: $1.50
- I stand and walk quietly in line: $1.75
- I help my classmates: $2.50
- I keep my work area and desk neat: $2

The areas in which your students need to show improvement should have a high value. For instance, if your students are continuously submitting sloppy work and keeping their desks messy, give them an example of how you want their work and desks to look. Then assign a high value to neatly submitted work and well-maintained desks.

Each student should be given a small storage bag to keep his or her "money." At the end of the day, the students can deposit the money in the bank. A chart will maintain student account balances. At the end of the week, students can shop at the classroom store to buy various goods and services with the money they have earned.

Consequences

The consequences of this system are a verbal warning, a written warning, monetary loss (e.g., the student loses 50¢–$1 for continuing to break a particular rule) and, finally, contacting the student's parent or a trip to the front office.

Materials

The materials needed for this system are:

- small storage bags
- fake money
- a dry erase board to write student account balances
- items for the classroom store

GROUP PLANS

Points Board

Procedures

The students will be divided into groups. Each group will have a name that the group members select. Each group will earn points for following the classroom rules and any behavioral objectives you want to improve upon. Points will be given in one- to five-point increments.

As with the Classroom Cash system, compile a list of objectives that you want to work on in conjunction with the classroom rules. Assign a value to each rule and objective. Each group should be given a typed, laminated copy of the rules and objectives, and their values. It is important to create rules and objectives that are team builders. Listed below are examples of team-building behavioral objectives:

- We make sure everyone in the group is following instructions: 5 points
- We help our group mates keep their areas neat: 3 points
- When one of our group mates is having a bad day, we use kind words to cheer him or her up: 5 points
- We make sure everyone in the group is on task: 3 points
- We make sure everyone in the group has turned in neat, well-done work: 4 points

The points will be recorded in the form of tally marks on a large dry erase board kept at the front of the classroom. A representative from each table should record points as they are earned for the table. If an individual earns points for his or her table, verbally recognize the student's accomplishment and have the table representative record the points.

Students should be told the weekly goal on Mondays. The goal should be written at the bottom of the board in large script. At the end of the week, count the number of points earned and distribute the weekly reward to the groups that earned it.

Consequences

The consequences of this system are a verbal warning, a written warning, loss of points (e.g., the group loses one to two points when a student continues to break a particular rule) and, finally, contacting the student's parent or a trip to the front office.

Materials

The materials needed for this system are:

- a large dry erase board
- dry erase pens
- weekly rewards

Group Modified Classroom Cash System

Procedures

In this system, which is most advantageous for upper elementary grades, groups serve as companies. Each company will have its own name and bank account, and the students will work toward earning money for the company. Rewards should be distributed on a biweekly or monthly basis when the students shop at the classroom store.

Consequences

The consequences of this system are a verbal warning, a written warning, loss of money (e.g., the company loses $1 when a student continues to break a particular rule) and, finally, contacting the student's parent or a trip to the front office.

Materials

The materials for this system are:

- fake money
- items for the classroom store
- a dry erase board
- dry erase pens
- storage bags

Children with disabilities or special needs will be mainstreamed into your classroom. Along with your behavior management system, you will need to incorporate additional strategies to ensure their academic success. The Quiet Corner and Letting Out My Feelings Book/Daily Classroom Journal are two such strategies; others include the "stoplight," breathing techniques, and the calming music station.

The "stoplight" consists of a laminated drawing of a stoplight, with red, yellow, and green circles as lights. Place a piece of VELCRO® in the center of each colored circle, and make a name tag for each student that has a corresponding VELCRO® fastener attached to its back.

When the student feels that all is well and that he or she understands the topics at hand, he or she should fasten his or her name tag to the green light. If the student begins to feel frustrated or anxious, he or she should fasten his or her name to the yellow light, and when he or she cannot go any further and absolutely needs help, the name tag should be fastened to the red light.

The stoplight is wonderful for students who have difficulty expressing themselves. For instance, students with Asperger's Syndrome, severe speech issues, and emotional problems will have a way to communicate clearly to you how they feel. Before implementing this in your classroom, clearly explain to the student what each color represents. Give the students scenarios of when each color should be used. When this strategy is first implemented, you will have to assist the student in using the stoplight until he or she can do so independently.

Breathing techniques are incorporated to teach the student how to calm down. Explain to the student that whenever he or she is feeling overwhelmed or is on the verge of a meltdown, he or she should take long breaths. This strategy requires your guidance. Speak to the student in a soft tone and tell him or her to breathe in deeply and exhale very slowly. You will have to model and prompt the student to use this strategy until he or she can do it independently.

The calming music station can be part of your Quiet Corner. Calming music is instrumental music usually heard in spas. Buy an inexpensive portable CD player and at least three spa music CDs and place them in the Quiet Corner.

Whenever your special needs student feels anxious or upset, send him or her to the Quiet Corner to listen to a CD. The student should set the silent timer for five minutes. Limit the use of the station to no more than twice a day.

After your special needs student has used the stoplight, breathing techniques, or calming music station to indicate and relieve frustrations he or she may feel, help the student come up with a plan of action to go forward with the rest of the day. You should ask the student to pinpoint what is upsetting or frustrating him or her. Once that is established, help the student think of ways to solve the problem.

In this chapter, examples of individual and group plans were given. The Stamp Card and Classroom Cash are examples of individual plans, while the Points Board and Modified Classroom Cash are examples of group plans. The Classroom Cash system is an example of a behavior system that can be used as both an individual and group system. For students with special needs, additional techniques, such as the "stoplight," breathing techniques, and the calming music station may be used in conjunction with your behavior plan.

QUICK TIPS

- Talk to your school guidance counselor about additional coping techniques to incorporate in your classroom.
- If you teach a student with Asperger's Syndrome or any other type of autism, check to see if your school system has an autism specialist. This person will be a great resource about other strategies to use in your classroom.

Time Block	Monday	Tuesday	Wednesday	Thursday	Friday
Morning Start-Up					
Language Arts					
Specials					
Math					
Science and Social Studies					

Objectives:

1. I will raise my hand to share.
2. I will follow an instruction the first time it is given.
3. I will show respect to everyone in the class.
4. I will stay on task the entire time.
5. I will listen while others are talking.

Weekly Goal: _____ stamps **Parent Signature:** _____

Stamp Card Template

10

The Universal Behavior Plan

Your teaching experience will include students with behavioral issues. The behavior management system you created may not be enough. In cases like this, the universal behavior plan should be implemented. The purpose of the universal behavior plan is to:

- target and reduce specific inappropriate behaviors
- increase specific positive behaviors
- ensure continuity of expectations and reinforcement at:
    - school
    - home
    - tutoring (if applicable)
    - speech (if applicable)
    - occupational therapy sessions (if applicable)

In order to design and successfully implement a universal behavior plan, you must:

- initially target three specific behaviors
- create no more than three consequences

- set a weekly points goal (the universal behavior plan is a points-based system)
- decide, in conjunction with the parents, the weekly reward; create "points cards" and a "points bank"
- design and institute coping techniques
- set a time line
- clearly explain the implementation of the plan to caregivers verbally and in writing

Before creating the plan, meet with the student's parents and any other caregivers, such as tutors or therapists. Ask each of them to select three specific inappropriate behaviors displayed by the student that the caregiver would like to reduce. For each of these behaviors, identify the opposite appropriate behavior.

For instance, if the student shares thoughts or feelings at home by constantly yelling, the opposite appropriate behavior is that the student shares by using his or her inside voice. The appropriate behaviors should be positively stated on the "points cards" as objectives.

The behaviors selected must be specific. Some examples of specific inappropriate behaviors are not completing a task the first time the student is given the instruction, interrupting when others are talking, snatching, and talking back.

After the appropriate behaviors are selected, consequences must be created. I recommend three consequences and no more. The first consequence should be a verbal warning. As discussed earlier, when issuing warnings, engage the student in the process by asking him or her which behavioral objective he or she is not reaching. Then ask the student what he or she can do to get back on track to reach the objective.

The second consequence should be a written warning. Give the student a laminated strip of paper that reads "WARNING! I am not reaching my objectives." If the inappropriate behavior is being repeated, point this out to the student and ask why. At this point, the child may be on the verge of losing points.

Advise the student of this and assist him or her in coming up with a plan to get back on track. After the plan is made, verbally praise the child for following it. Take the WARNING card away after a few instances of the student's following the plan.

The final consequence is to take away points in one- to two-point increments. Let the student know the number of points he or she has lost. Ask the student why the points were lost. Then have him or her erase the specified number of points. Afterward, ask the student how he or she can earn the points back.

Each week, decide with the parents what the weekly points goal will be. I propose beginning with 50 points. This amount allows the student to work toward an attainable goal. The points accrued during the week at school, home, and any other place the plan is to be implemented will be entered in a "points bank." Each week of the plan, increase the weekly goal by 10 to 20 points.

The weekly rewards, if the goal is met, will be given by the parents. At your initial meeting, brainstorm with the parents to create a list of rewards. Rank the rewards from lowest to highest, and have the parents distribute points to the student weekly using that ranking.

The weekly points cards should list the:

- days of the week
- positive behaviors chosen as behavioral objectives
- consequences
- weekly goal
- weekly reward

A points card should be made for school, home, and any other place the plan will be used. At the end of the week, the points cards should be sent home for the student and his or her parents to total all the points.

Along with the points cards is the points bank. The parents will enter the accrued points into the bank and distribute the weekly reward if the goal has been reached.

Sometimes the student will have difficulty reaching his or her behavioral objectives. Create various simple coping techniques that can be used to calm him or her down when this happens. Examples of coping techniques are taking deep breaths, counting backward, using a clicker for a prescribed amount of time, and going to a quiet area for three to five minutes.

A time frame should be created to allow the caregivers a specified amount of time to enforce the plan. The plan should be put into action in five- to six-week cycles. At the end of this time frame, meet with the caregivers.

If the student has reached his or her behavioral objectives, select four more target behaviors and repeat the process. However, during this five- to six-week cycle, the student will be given rewards every two weeks. As time progresses, increase the number of objectives and the time frame in which rewards will be distributed. If the student has not reached his or her behavioral objectives, extend the time frame and discuss alternatives with your school's guidance counselor or principal.

Before implementing the plan, meet with all the caregivers at the same time and clearly explain the plan. Discuss verbal praise and redirecting with the caregivers. Also, give the caregivers scenarios and model the types of responses they should have as well as a written copy of the plan. A detailed example of a universal behavior plan, along with the templates for a points card and a points bank, is provided below.

In order for the universal behavior plan to be effective, there must be clear communication between all caregivers and consistency. The plan is regimented and requires diligence and patience in order to see results. All parties involved must be fully committed to its success.

UNIVERSAL BEHAVIOR PLAN

Purpose

The purpose of this behavior plan is to provide the student with a consistent behavior system that reinforces positive behavior. This plan is to be used at home, school, therapy, and tutoring sessions.

Plan
- The positive behaviors that the system will reinforce will be stated as objectives outlined on the "points card."
- The student will have three points cards: one for home, one for school, and one for tutoring and therapy sessions.
- For each card, the student will have three objectives to begin with; as the year progresses, the number will be extended to five objectives.
- The student will also have a "points bank" that will track the number of points he or she accrues weekly.
- The points the student accrues during his or her speech, tutoring, OT sessions, and school will be transferred home and recorded in the points bank.
- At the end of the week, all of the student's points should be added to see if the weekly goal has been reached.
- The student should carry his or her tutoring and therapy sessions card whenever he or she goes to receive these services.
- On Fridays, the student should bring the school points card home so that the points earned during the school week can be tallied.
- At the beginning of this system, the student will have a "weekly goal" of how many points he or she needs to earn in order to receive the "weekly reward."
- The weekly goal and weekly reward will be written at the bottom of each card.
- When introducing the system to the student, read each of the objectives aloud to him or her and have the student repeat each objective.
- Discuss ways the student can reach each objective by giving examples and scenarios in which he or she can earn points.
- Ask the student questions to ensure that he or she clearly understands each objective.
- Also discuss the consequences with the student. (See Consequences section for further explanation.)

- Each time the student reaches one of his or her daily objectives, he or she should be given points in three- to five-point increments represented as tally marks.
- The student can reach an objective several times within a session or time period.
- The purpose of this system is to constantly "catch him or her being good" or reaching his or her objective. Every time the student reaches a goal, give him or her points.
- When beginning this behavior system, it is always advisable to be generous with points. This allows the student to see that his or her goals are attainable.
- When recording the points, allow the student to record some of the points to enable empowerment.
- With this system, you can take away points as well. Do this sparingly, as the purpose is to reinforce the positive behaviors outlined in the goals.
- As time progresses, the number of weekly points the student needs to earn must increase (e.g., his or her weekly goal for week 1 might be 50 points and for week 2 might be 65 points).
- As the weekly goals increase, the student will have to work harder to earn points but should always be given positive verbal reinforcement—catch the student being good!

Timeline for Plan
- The plan is to be used in six-week spans.
- For the first six-week span, the student will have three objectives for each card and will receive weekly rewards.
- For the second six-week span, the student will have four goals for each card and will receive rewards every two weeks (he or she will have two weeks, rather than one week, to earn points).
- For the third six-week span, the student will have five goals for each card and will receive rewards every three weeks (he or she will have three weeks, rather than two weeks, to earn points).

- For the fourth six-week span, the student will have six goals for each card and will receive rewards monthly (he or she will have four weeks, rather than three weeks, to earn points).
- The points bank card will change to reflect how the student will earn points, as explained above.
- The aforementioned time line depends on how well the student reaches his or her goals.

Objectives
- The objectives for home will be as follows (but can easily be changed):
  - I used good manners by saying please, thank you, and you're welcome.
  - I completed a task after being told only once to do it.
  - I used my inside voice when talking to others.
- The objectives for school, tutoring, and therapy sessions will be different, depending on what each adult wants to work on.
- Objectives should always be stated positively.
- You and the caregivers should meet at the end of each time span to change, adjust, or add goals.
- Once the student has successfully accomplished an objective without having to be reminded to exercise the behavior, that objective can be replaced with another.

Implementation
- In order for this system to work, everyone must be consistent and diligent in reinforcing the positive behaviors.
- When the student reaches an objective, verbally recognize that he or she reached the objective and tell him or her how many points he or she will earn. For example, you might say, "I like the way you used good manners by saying thank you, so you have earned two points."

THE UNIVERSAL BEHAVIOR PLAN

- As the plan progresses, you can increase the amount of points earned each time an objective is reached.

Consequences
- If the student is not following instructions, his or her consequences will be as follows:

  - Verbal Warning: for instance, if the student is yelling and one of the objectives is to use his or her inside voice, say, "Are you using your inside voice by yelling? This is your verbal warning; from now on, use your inside voice."
  - Written Warning: for example, give the student the laminated WARNING card. You might say, "You are yelling again. If it happens again, you will lose two points. What can you do to get back on track?"
  - The final consequence is to take away points. When taking away points, let the student know specifically what he or she is doing to lose the points and how many points he or she will lose. Also, always allow the student the opportunity to regain points; for instance, you might say, "You are still yelling and not using your inside voice. I have given you two warnings. Now you have lost two points. You can earn these points back by using your inside voice instead of yelling. You can also earn points by using good manners and following instructions the first time they are given."
  - When instructing the student on how he or she can earn points back, always verbally correct the negative behavior with a positive behavior and reiterate the other goals that will allow him or her the opportunity to earn points. An example of this was given in the point above.
  - Always use a soft tone.
  - If the student is angry, use some coping techniques to prevent the behavior from escalating.

Coping Techniques

If a student gets angry, it is best to use different coping techniques to calm him or her down. For example:

- Have the student take deep breaths.
- Lower your voice as the student gets louder.
- Give the student a clicker to click for a prescribed amount of time (e.g., 10 clicks).
- Provide a quiet corner with a timer where the student can calm down (but not play with toys or games); the timer should be set for no more than two to three minutes.

Rewards
- Rewards can be anything from a toy to a trip.
- At the beginning of the system, it is best to use small rewards such as a toy truck or action figure.
- As the system progresses toward triweekly (every three weeks) and monthly rewards, the rewards should be greater, like meeting the fire chief or going on a tour of the fire station.
- The points bank and points cards allow the student to see what he or she is working toward.
- Tell the student that it is always best to have more points than he or she needs, so the weekly goal can be exceeded.
- Listed below are examples of weekly rewards:
    - Trips to local museums
    - Trips to a local eatery, like McDonald's®
    - Extra play time or free time
    - Books
    - A day at work with Mom or Dad
    - A movie
    - An opportunity to go to the fire station

- A trip to the toy store to choose a toy (let the student know in advance how many points he or she must earn as a goal to obtain a given toy)

In this chapter, we discussed the universal behavior plan. The plan should be implemented when a student has difficulty adhering to the behavior management system put in place. In order for the plan to be effective, all parties involved must participate fully.

QUICK TIPS

- Ensure that all the participants in the plan have your e-mail address and phone number.
- Contact the participants of the plan on a weekly basis to listen to any comments and answer any questions.
- Always encourage the participants in the plan to keep the student motivated.

Home Points Card

Objective	Sunday	Monday	Tuesday	Wednesday	Thursday	Friday	Saturday
I completed a task after being told only once to do it.							
I used good manners by saying please, thank you, and you're welcome.							
I used my inside voice when talking to others.							

Weekly Goal: _____ Points
Weekly Reward: _____
Consequences: 1. Verbal Warning 2. Written Warning 3. Take away points

Home Points Card

Tutoring & Therapy Sessions Card

Objective	Sunday	Monday	Tuesday	Wednesday	Thursday	Friday	Saturday
I followed an instruction the first time it was given.							
I stayed on task the entire time I was completing a task.							
I used my inside voice when talking to others.							

Weekly Goal: _____ Points   Weekly Reward: _____
Consequences: 1. Verbal Warning   2. Written Warning   3. Take away points

Tutoring and Therapy Sessions Card

Points Bank

Week 1	Week 2	Week 3	Week 4	Week 5
I earned ___ points in Speech, Tutoring and OT.	I earned ___ points in Speech, Tutoring and OT.	I earned ___ points in Speech, Tutoring and OT.	I earned ___ points in Speech, Tutoring and OT.	I earned ___ points in Speech, Tutoring and OT.
I earned ___ points at home.	I earned ___ points at home.	I earned ___ points at home.	I earned ___ points at home.	I earned ___ points at home.
I earned ___ points at school.	I earned ___ points at school.	I earned ___ points at school.	I earned ___ points at school.	I earned ___ points at school.
Grand Total: ___ points	Grand Total: ___ points	Grand Total: ___ points	Grand Total: ___ points	Grand Total: ___ points

Points Bank

Recommended Readings

READING

The Art of Teaching Reading by Lucy McCormick Calkins. ISBN: 0-321-08059-9.

Building Academic Vocabulary: Teacher's Manual by Robert Marzano. ISBN: 978-1-416-60234-7.

Guided Reading: Good First Teaching for All Children by Irene Fountas and Gay Su Pinnell. ISBN: 0-435-08863-7.

Guiding Readers and Writers: Teaching Comprehension, Genre, and Content Literacy by Irene Fountas and Gay Su Pinnell. ISBN: 978-0-325-00310-8.

In the Middle: New Understanding About Writing, Reading and Learning by Nancie Atwell. ISBN: 0-867-09374-9.

Making Content Comprehensible: The SIOP Model for English Learners by Jana Echevarria. ISBN: 978-0-205-51886-9.

Phonics From A to Z: A Practical Guide by Wiley Blevins. ISBN: 978-0-439-84511-3.

The Reading Teacher's Book of Lists by Edward B. Fry and Jacqueline E. Kress. ISBN: 0-787-98257-1.

Reading with Meaning: Teaching Comprehension in the Primary Grades by Debbie Miller. ISBN: 978-1-571-10307-9.

Small-Group Reading Instruction: A Differentiated Teaching Model for Intermediate Readers, Grades 3–8 by Beverly Tyner and Sharon Green. ISBN: 0-872-07574-5.

Strategies That Work: Teaching Comprehension for Understanding and Engagement by Stephanie Harvey and Anne Goudvis. ISBN: 978-1-571-10481-6.
Tools for Teaching Content Literacy by Janet Allen. ISBN: 978-1-571-10380-2.
Word Journeys: Assessment-Guided Phonics, Spelling, and Vocabulary Instruction by Kathy Ganske. ISBN: 1-572-30559-2.
Word Matters: Teaching Phonics and Spelling in the Reading/Writing Classroom by Irene Fountas and Gay Su Pinnell. ISBN: 0-325-00051-4.
Word Sorts and More: Sound, Pattern, and Meaning Explorations K–3 by Kathy Ganske. ISBN: 978-1-593-85050-0.
Words Their Way: Word Study for Phonics Vocabulary by Donald Bear, Marcia Invernizzi, Francine Johnston, and Shane Templeton. ISBN: 978-0-132-23968-4.

WRITING

15 Easy Lessons That Build Basic Writing Skills in Grades K–2 by Mary Rose. ISBN: 978-0-439-27163-9.
25 Mini-Lessons for Teaching Writing (Grades 3–6) by Adele Fiderer. ISBN: 978-0-590-20940-3.
100 Trait Specific Comments: A Quick Guide for Giving Constructive Feedback on Student Writing by Ruth Culham. ISBN: 978-0-439-79602-6.
About the Authors: Writing Workshop with Our Youngest Writers by Lisa Cleveland and Katie Wood Ray. ISBN: 978-0-325-00511-9.
The Art of Teaching Writing by Lucy Calkins. ISBN: 978-0-435-08809-5.
Instant Independent Reading Response Activities by Laura Witmer. ISBN: 978-0-439-30961-5.
Mechanically Inclined: Building Grammar, Usage, and Style into Writer's Workshop by Jeff Anderson and Vicki Spandel. ISBN: 978-1-571-10412-0.
The Most Wonderful Writing Lessons Ever (Grades 2–4) by Barbara Mariconda. ISBN: 978-0-590-87304-8.
Planning for Successful Reading and Writing Instruction in K–2 by Antoinette Forshnell. ISBN: 978-0-439-36593-2.
Step-by-Step Strategies for Teaching Expository Writing by Barbara Mariconda. ISBN: 978-0-439-26081-7.

Super Story-Writing Strategies and Activities (Grades 3–6) by Barbara Mariconda. ISBN: 978-0-439-14008-9.

Using Picture Books to Teach Writing with the Traits by Ruth Culham. ISBN: 0-439-55687-2.

Wondrous Words: Writers and Writing in the Elementary Classroom by Katie Wood Ray. ISBN: 0-814-15816-1.

A Writer's Notebook: Unlocking the Writer within You by Ralph Fletcher. ISBN: 978-0-380-78430-1.

The Writing Workshop: Working through the Hard Parts (And They're All Hard Parts) by Katie Wood Ray and Lester Laminack. ISBN: 978-0-814-11317-2.

DIFFERENTIATION

Differentiated Instructional Strategies for Reading in the Content Areas by Carolyn Chapman and Rita S. King. ISBN: 978-0-761-93825-5.

Differentiation in Practice: A Resource Guide for Differentiating Curriculum, Grades K–5 by Carol Ann Tomlinson and Carol Cunningham Eidson. ISBN: 978-0-871-20760-9.

How to Differentiate Instruction in Mixed-Ability Classrooms by Carol Ann Tomlinson. ISBN: 978-0-871-20512-4.

Making It Work: Differentiated Instruction by Patti Drapeau. ISBN: 978-0-439-51778-2.

Making the Most of Small Groups: Differentiation for All by Debbie Diller. ISBN: 978-1-571-10431-1.

TECHNOLOGY

1001 Best Websites for Educators by Timothy Hopkins. ISBN: 978-0-743-93877-8.

Blogs, Wikis, Podcasts, and Other Powerful Web Tools for Classrooms by Will Richardson. ISBN: 1-412-92767-6.

Engaging the Online Leaner: Actvities and Resources for Creative Instruction by Rita-Marie Conrad. ISBN: 0-787-96667-3.

Meaningful Learning with Technology by David H. Jonassen, Jane Howland, Rose M. Marra, and David Crismond. ISBN: 0-132-39395-6.

Podcasting for Teachers: Using a New Technology to Revolutionize Teaching and Learning by Kathleen King. ISBN: 1-593-11658-6.

MATH

50 Problem-Solving Lessons: The Best from 10 Years of Math Solutions Newsletters by Marilyn Burns. ISBN: 978-0-941-35516-2.

About Teaching Mathematics: A K–8 Resource by Marilyn Burns. ISBN: 978-0-941-35576-6.

Comprehending Math: Adapting Reading Strategies to Teach Mathematics, K–6 by Arthur Hyde. ISBN: 978-0-941-35551-3.

Differentiating Math Instruction: Strategies That Work for K–8 Classrooms! by William N. Bender. ISBN: 978-0-761-93148-5.

Learning Through Problems: Number Sense and Computational Strategies/A Resource for Primary Teachers by Paul Trafton. ISBN: 978-0-325-00126-5.

Lessons for Algebraic Thinking: Grades 3–5 by Maryann Wickett. ISBN: 978-0-941-35548-3.

Math and Literature: Grades 4–6 by Rusty Bresser. ISBN: 978-0-941-35568-1.

Math and Nonfiction: Grades K–2 by Jamee Petersen. ISBN: 978-0-941-35561-2.

Teaching Student-Centered Mathematics: Grades K–3 by John Van de Walle and Lou Ann H. Lovin. ISBN: 978-0-205-40843-6.

Writing in Math Class: A Resource for Grades 2–8 by Marilyn Burns. ISBN: 978-0-941-35513-1.

MISCELLANEOUS

Activities That Teach by Tom Jackson. ISBN: 0-916-09549-5.

The Complete Guide to Asperger's Syndrome by Tony Attwood. ISBN: 1-84310-669-8.

How to Handle Difficult Parents: A Teacher's Survival Guide by Suzanne Capek Tingley. ISBN: 1-877-67372-2.

Literacy Work Stations: Making Centers Work by Debbie Diller. ISBN: 1-571-10353-8.

The Morning Meeting Book (Strategies for Teachers) by Roxann Kriete. ISBN: 1-892-98909-3.

Index

administrative duties, 13, 35–36

Back-to-School Night, 39, 45, 47, 51
behavioral objectives, 115–18, 120–24, 132–33
Bloom's Taxonomy, 53, 61–64
breathing techniques, 126–28
bulletin boards, 3, 18–19, 22, 25, 32

calming music station, 126–28
centers, 3–6, 9–11, 13, 19–20
classroom library, 3, 6, 10–11, 19, 96
completed-work trays, 26, 30, 36
components of a lesson plan, 53–57
consequences: creating, 100, 115, 120–21, 124–26, 130–31, 137; enforcing, 103–4, 118–21, 134, 137; posting, 16, 102–3, 117, 132
coping techniques, 128, 131, 133, 137–38
cross-curricular units, 53, 65–66

daily checklists, 26, 30, 33, 37, 39, 42
daily routine: student, 14, 29–30, 32, 93–97; teacher, 35–37, 39, 41–42
dead time, 29, 93, 97
differentiated activities, 4, 41, 53, 60, 66
documentation, 35, 38–39, 45, 50, 122

five-finger rule, 11

goals: behavioral, 115, 117, 119–20, 122, 135–37; lesson plans, 53–55, 57, 78
grading, 20, 35–36, 43–44, 50

homework management, 18, 20, 26, 31–33, 35, 43, 47, 50, 95

intervention strategies, 37
introductory letter, 51–52

learning objectives, 3–4, 16, 37–38, 40, 60
learning styles: auditory, 4, 60; tactile/kinesthetic, 4–5, 7, 60; visual, 4, 60
lesson plan book, 22, 35, 40–41, 57
Letting Out My Feelings/Daily Classroom Journal, 6–7, 102, 126

make-up work, 35, 43, 47, 50
"making it right," 100, 103–4
math center, 9–10

negative reinforcement, 108, 110–11

observations, 35, 40–42, 54
organization of desk/work space: student, 26, 30, 33, 117–18, 123; teacher, 35, 39–41

parent: communication, 31, 35–39, 43, 45–49, 51–52, 64, 102, 108–9, 120, 122, 124–26, 131, 132; volunteers, 35, 49, 69
parent-teacher conferences, 39, 47–49
pencil boxes, 22, 26, 28–29, 96
positive reinforcement, 41, 108–9, 111, 135

Quiet Corner, 3, 12–13, 102, 126–27, 138

researching topics, 53, 64
rewards, 34, 109–11, 115–17, 119, 122, 125–26, 132–33, 135–36, 138

routines, 14, 27, 29–30, 32, 35–37, 39, 41–42, 44–45, 93, 97
rubrics, 36, 44, 53, 65–66, 89
rules: creating, 12–13, 41, 99–100, 104, 115, 124; enforcing, 4, 12–13, 100–103, 105–6, 117–21, 124; posting, 3, 12–13, 16, 41, 102–3, 117, 121, 124

scenarios, 107
schedules, 3, 16, 27, 44, 47, 50, 93–95, 110
seating, 3, 14–15, 44, 51
shopping list, 13, 20–24, 28–31, 36
simple procedures, 93, 97
stoplight, 126–28
storage areas, 3, 13, 19
student organizers, 28, 33–34
substitute letter, 50–51
substitute plans, 35, 44–45

take-home folders, 26, 31–32, 122
teacher development, 35, 42, 65
technology, 53, 64–65, 145–46

volunteers, 35, 37, 49, 58, 69, 74

weekly jobs and responsibilities, 5, 18, 26, 32
word wall, 3, 5, 9–10, 38
work examples, 7, 26, 29, 33, 43, 48, 56
writing process, 7–9, 10–11, 74

About the Author

L. K. Masao received a Bachelor of Science degree in Elementary Education from the College of Charleston and a Master of Education degree from The George Washington University Graduate School of Education and Human Development. She has taught in northern Virginia's Alexandria City Public Schools at a traditional academy.